A Year in Connemara

A YEAR
IN
CONNEMARA

Guy St John Williams

DALETTA PRESS

Published by

DALETTA PRESS

PO BOX 47 MONASTEREVAN CO KILDARE
PHONE/FAX 045 523449

Line drawings by Hugh Webster

Design and print origination by O'K Graphic Design, Dublin

Printed in Ireland by ColourBooks Ltd, Dublin

This book is typeset in 11/15 pt Cochin

To all habitués of Heather Island, past and present

Some of the names in this narrative may be fictitious, but then many of the characters are surreal.

July

~~~

"What have you heard from Singapore?" was the question that interrupted my reverie, as I watched the endless traffic streaming across the Taipa bridge, that miracle of Portuguese engineering which was now well past its allotted lifespan. My lady wife is slim, blonde and strikingly aquiline. The elegance of her features is occasionally offset by a peremptory mode of address. She had taken to the Orient as a duck to water, enchanted and alarmed in turn by Cantonese customs.

"I've got an interview organised to coincide with our return home at the end of June." How could I tell Milady that my mind was made up? No more Macau. No Singapore. No more professional involvement in horseracing, in whatever guise. I was going home, and "home" in this instance was a semi-derelict house on an island, in a lake, in farthest Connemara, "the last parish before New York". The house was full of bats, and the lake stiff with brown trout. I would be there in a week or so.

Born into a large family business in the Irish midlands, its fortunes founded and dissipated in whiskey, I had forsaken a marketing career for the rollercoaster of racehorse training. When the lows eventually outweighed the highs I had gone to work for the Jockey Club in England, based in the pastoral splendours of North Yorkshire — Ireland with Money. That pleasant existence had come to an acrimonious end some years later, to be followed by a period of desultory, dilettante dealing in the finer things in life, such as books and paintings and furniture; reluctant to leave Yorkshire, yet with no real reason to remain there. Yorkshire simply wasn't "home".

My stint with the English Jockey Club — irrespective of its outcome — had made me eligible for expatriate employment in similar positions. As yet unwilling to eschew completely the security of salaried employment, I had signed on with the Macau Jockey Club, an uneasy alliance of Triads and Taiwanese. In a situation where races must never be rigged, but the outcome should always be known beforehand to "Management", it was only the unpredictability of the horses themselves that preserved any element of chance. Even this imponderable had become almost eliminated by the stealthy influx of Antipodeans. The unwholesome confluence of Cantonese chicanery and Antipodean avarice left no room for "sportsmen" in this hotbed of corruption. It was time to leave.

An initial, tentative foray to the Lion City had not entirely convinced me that Singapore constituted a worthwhile "career move", even if I had ever envisaged racing officialdom as a career, per se. Wined and dined by a Chinee, I had been tested by my host. "You find yourself confwonted by a wattlesnake and an Indian. You have one bullet in your pistol. Which do you shoot dead?" Uneasy silence, in unknown company ... "Simple! You kill the Indian, for he is the most deadly." And I should seek employment in Singapore? Two chances! If Macau had been an aberration — admittedly a fascinating one — what purpose could be served by continuing this expatriate existence, living well, but forever displaced?

That starless night on our balcony in Macau I resolved to go home, and let the future take care of itself. You only go round once, and while I do not live every day as though it were my last, I do believe that life is for living. Too many of my "successful" acquaintances have failed to make old bones.

George Moore, who "sacrificed his country and friends for art's sake", once wrote: "A man travels the world over in search of what he needs, and returns home to find it." Milady had given me that quotation on a card. She adores cards and I relish the writings of George Moore. Thus do marriages endure.

The leaving of Macau was even more efficient than its occupation. We listed and priced our artefacts, circulated the list among the handful of "gweilo" expatriates, and flogged the lot. Bereft of all that we had acquired, but briefly in funds, we were free to leave. And did, by hangover and hydrofoil to Hongkong, the crossroads of Southeast Asia. Relinquishing the clamour and the oriental odours of "magical Hongkong" through the frozen air-conditioning of Kai Tak, we headed to Singapore. The Lion City lay two hours to the west — a step in the right direction, homewards.

My interview was perfunctory, uncommitted, inconclusive, all that I had hoped. For all that the other expats wished me luck in my application to become part of the "team" in that fetid, equatorial steambath, I knew it was not to be. It was not for me. Besides, our twins were about to start their secondary education, preferably in an Irish ethos.

Our onward journey took us to Manchester, where it was raining. But Yorkshire — North Yorkshire, that magnificent spread of country beyond the dank, forbidding Pennines — was at its finest. The sun shone, the wine flowed and winners were childishly simple to back on the Knavesmire. Not. indeed, that I would advocate betting on horses in races; just that life itself is not greatly dissimilar.

It was very, very tempting to re-root where we had been so happy. But why? Yorkshire was not "home"; and "home" was where I was determined to be. Milady and our eleven-year-old twins needed no second bidding to stay amongst friends. I could head to Connemara, with all our bags and baggage in the durable Vauxhall Cavalier, my severance souvenir of six years with the Jockey Club.

"To travel hopefully is a better thing than to arrive, and the true success is to labour." The first part of this maxim I had been brought up to attribute to that venerated Chinee, Confucius, whence derives the term "confusion". The addendum — it transpires — is an observation of that adoptive Samoan, Robert Louis Stevenson. It hardly rings true of Robinson Crusoe; still less of Man Friday. Both parts were destined to apply — on my Treasure Island ...

The journey to my goal, that had started in sweltering Macau, only took on real meaning as I drove into Oughterard, the Corrib-side fishing village that styles itself "the gateway to Connemara". Bounded on the east by the graveyard that Joyce featured in his story "The Dead" and on the west by Clare Villa, home to George Bernard Shaw's mother, Oughterard was indeed once the "gateway" to the most extensive estate in these islands, the 200,000-acre fiefdom of the Martins and asylum to all manner of rogues, raparees and revolutionaries. "Humanity Dick" Martin once observed to his good friend, George IV, that the only writ that ran in Connemara belonged not to His Majesty, but to Martin.

The sudden vista of rock and bog, sky and mountain, space and freedom made my heart lurch, like an unexpected encounter with a lover. The telegraph poles teeter tipsily into the distance, like a rout of exhausted climbers, roped together for mutual survival. The last great wilderness in Europe, with its vestiges of the long-vanished railway line, was all now that lay between me and Heather Island. On and on through lakes innumerable — Shindilla, Glendollagh and Derryclare — skirting the biggest of them all, Lough Inagh, sometime Mecca for seatrout anglers. After a year away I would have to learn again how to "read" the sheep that wander the roads; which would dart across my path and which would continue unconcernedly grazing "God's acre", amid the blazing gorse. The lunar landscape of the Inagh valley abruptly gave way to the lush afforestation of Kylemore, that Gothic extravaganza created by Manchester millionaire Mitchell Henry and now a Benedictine Abbey.

The three-pub crossroads of Letterfrack signalled the beginning of the end of my journey. Time to buy the essentials of existence in Connemara's Hudson Bay Trading Post, selling everything from drink to cattle drench. The Charolais bull stood patiently in his trailer behind the Gateaux van. Only the real thing for Connemara cows. "Welcome, Sir Guy!" The proprietor rubbed his hands, in eager expectation of our renewed custom over the coming weeks. The morning coffee drinkers seemed hearteningly familiar, as though I had never been away. Terry with his half-smoked cheroot, Gerry Park with his roll-ups, Alastair in his chef's gear, Oisín shambling around in search of some particular vantage point, the "Squire", "Sam Sailor" and Lil, the doyenne, on her special stool. My conversational gambit — "How's the fishing been?" — brought a suitably cryptic response: "There's few enough comin' up by river, but a quare number by road." I knew I was back.

The final four miles took me twisting and swooping along that switchback through Derryinver, Tullycross and Tully, left by the Teach Ceoil and thence to our laneway, blocked for the moment by Martin Golden's tractor and trailer. Martin was moving sheep from his field that flanks our lane, while, on the opposite side, Thady Hurley tended his immaculate garden, a labour of love in surroundings where the very air is laden with salt from the Atlantic. Their greetings implied that I had been absent for a week or maybe two, putting the frenzies of other worlds into proper perspective. The departure of the bleating sheep left me free to continue down our rutted, potholed "avenue" to the boat house on the lakeshore. A pair of swans cruised the waters, as the curlews and seagulls swirled and cried above.

That there was nobody about did not really surprise. True, Malachy Kane, farmer, occasional builder and fanatical fisherman, had promised to turn up. Instead, he had left his boat (for he distrusted mine) tied up beside the little jetty. In due course I was to realise the reason for his non-appearance. At the time his gesture seemed fulfillment of a prophecy. Almost half a century ago my grandfather, who owned the place then, had written of his approach to Heather Island, in a piece entitled *Freilaun*.

"In Tully Lake there is an island eleven acres in extent called 'Freilaun', which means Heather Island. It lies midway between the nearest shores under the great rock of Letter Hill, which shelters it from the prevailing winds. The lake is shaped like a long oval which has been contracted near the middle where the island lies. On the eastern shore there is a garage which is also a boathouse. A boat is kept beside it by a little pier. A few minutes' rowing brings you to the island where the boat can run into a harbour the size of the boat. When you step ashore you are at the beginning of a path that winds crimson-walled by fuchsia, and roofed by laurel, rhododendrons and flowering shrubs. After thirty yards the air grows warmer because of a copse of linden and sycamore trees. Before you suddenly a long two-storeyed, lime-white house comes into view with a veranda of brown timber running along over the first storey. Between the house and the lindens is a little court paved with irregular slats, russet and brown and sea-green. The silence that reigns on the island may be broken only by a startled blackbird or a belted bee barging back, by and large, from a foray on the spreading flowers; or, in the long Spring, by a cuckoo that sounds as if it were close by. At evening a pair of wild pigeons make love-lorn moanings as they settle in the trees.

"A bank behind the house rises as high and shelters it with trees and shrubs from any breezes from the North. To the south the view is open over the lake to the Twelve Bens of Connemara, which seem quite near, though glistening Diamond Mountain, the nearest of them, is five miles away.

"On the ground floor every window gives on the green and purple of the rhododendrons or the pink of rambler roses crowding the garden wall. Over the lawn on the west side glimpses of the lake may be caught between the larger trees; but, though the house is in the middle of a lake, the lake-water is never heard lapping on the shore. It may be that the rowans, sallies and ivied trees that rim the lake keep away even the gentle sound of little waves.

"Where the lake itself preserves the silence, it is needless to say that the ambrosial night is not made hideous by the brayings of a radio.

"This is no place for the restlessness of youth; but a man well stepped in years it suits well."

Oliver St John Gogarty — my mother's father — had penned that description in Manhattan in 1950. It was published in a collection entitled *Rolling down the lea*. Freilaun had been his occasional hideaway, a place of refuge, commemorated lovingly in poetry and prose. Although he had, at one time, collected houses, and even castles, he had never considered Heather Island as his home. Was I foolish to attempt to outdo my distinguished forebear? Quite probably. I could still change my mind. It wasn't too late. They say it's never too late ...

Was it feminine wiles that prompted Milady to prolong her stay in Yorkshire, with the twins, Nicholas and Camellia? Did she perhaps hope that, left alone on Heather Island for a few days, I would come to my senses, realise the utter impracticability of self-imposed seclusion and set about securing "a proper job"? If that was her ploy, it almost succeeded.

Malachy's non-appearance had been no accident ... Of the various repairs he had contracted to do following our return to Macau the previous autumn, he had completed all but the most vital before the weather had broken. Basic internal work had been done, but the roof of the master bedroom had been left unfinished. It was reconstructed now, and right well it looked, dormer windows and all. But the contents, the furnishings, the drawingroom below ... too sodden even to burn.

Removing carpeting with a shovel isn't only back-breaking, it's soul-destroying. Still, the weather was fine, the days long and lots of hen pheasants and their newly-hatched broods for company. As a contribution to the local game club's efforts to establish pheasants as indigenous inhabitants of North Connemara, I had given the use of Heather Island as a rearing area and game sanctuary. In the absence of cats and dogs these pheasants had only water rats and sparrowhawks with which to contend. Even that, it transpired, was too much.

Perhaps I could get a telephone installed to greet Milady's arrival? Being half-American she has a fondness for instant communication, though protesting otherwise. Telecom Éireann played a blinder in this instance, promptly despatching their experienced "island team". Unusual among telecommunications engineers, these lads actively relished forays by boat to Inisbofin, Inisturk and the other islands off this rugged Atlantic coast. A lake island would be child's play, they told me.

Seán and Séamus duly arrived in their service van, followed down our pitted avenue by a lorry bearing a solitary pole. The pole was duly manhandled into the lake, tethered to the stern of my capricious little boat and towed across. With the pole safely tied to the island pier, the intrepid pair carried out their survey, swarming up and down the sturdy sycamores to establish the clearest line of transmission to the radio mast on Cregg, highest of the hills behind Clifden, our local town twelve miles to the south. Having pinpointed the optimum location and amputated a few obtruding branches, the lads dug the hole, erected the pole, topped it with its aerial, rigged up a battery at its base, ran a cable to the house, installed a 'phone and dialled the exchange. And just like that Heather Island was in touch with the world beyond the shores of Tully Lake.

Was it really that simple? No, it wasn't. The battery needed constant charging, normally obtained from adjacent supplies of mains electricity. But Heather Island hadn't got mains electricity ... though that was, of course, only a formality. In the meantime a generator would suffice. Seán—or was it Séamus?—just happened to know that Shane Ruane, in nearby Tully village, had recently acquired a job lot of petrol-driven generators, out of British Telecom trucks, as it happened. "Sure give him a ring, why don't you, now you've the 'phone!"

If I thought that my "nearest and dearest" was going to go into raptures at receiving a 'phone call from Heather Island, I was disappointed. Throughout a lifetime of summers spent down here we had managed perfectly well without telecommunications. Why did I now need such a facility, when we would be heading to sunnier climes in the autumn?

"Well, if I'm to get a job I must be contactable. And you can keep in touch with your friends."

"Hmmm. Pick us up in Galway airport. We land at lunchtime, a week from tomorrow."

Naturally inclined to look on the brighter side of any situation, I reckoned a week's grace could see a lot accomplished in the transformation of my semi-derelict abode. Anyway, its dereliction had come about by its always having been extraneous to its owners' needs. And that was no longer the case. On moving to Yorkshire some years before we had sold our house and training establishment outside Tullamore, which had been "home". Content to pay rent to Lord Howard de Walden for the privilege of living in the midst of a walled garden in the innermost recesses of his splendid Thornton Stud, where stood the most costly stallion in Europe at the time, we had never seriously contemplated buying a house of our own in England. So now we were effectively homeless. That awful spectre — to my mind at any rate — had always been more imagined than real. Didn't we own Heather Island, free and unencumbered?

With the master bedroom in devastation, my choices were narrowed to the five lesser boudoirs, all of which I had experienced at one time or another during my forty-something summers spent on Heather Island. I opted for the smallest, but warmest because it was directly above the bathstove in the hall, and thus closest to the solitary bathroom as well. As a child I had had the most vivid of nightmares in this room, running out of it shrieking in the dead of night. It had taken my bemused parents several nights to discover the cause. A barn owl had taken to alighting on my bedroom window and hooting into the darkness. My screams would banish him each time and it was only through an all-night vigil that cause and effect had eventually been established. But that had all happened many years ago and had never recurred. True, some few guests had claimed to see apparitions in the corridor and on the veranda. However, we had tended to be dismissive of their accounts, not wishing our own children to become alarmed.

It has long been held that a Jesuit education imbues a permanent sense of guilt. As a survivor of one such institution I am thus afflicted, which may explain my troubled night's sleep in the little bedroom beside the bathroom. I dreamt that I was in court, charged with the crime of rendering my family homeless. Outraged at such a preposterous accusation, I insisted on conducting my own defence. Heather Island, its surrounding lake and the house upon it belonged to me and constituted a perfectly adequate "home" for my wife and children. There simply was no case to answer, I asserted, before claiming damages arising from wrongful prosecution. I gazed defiantly around the courtroom, waiting airily for the judge to declare the case dismissed ...

"Does the counsel for the prosecution wish to question the defendant?" This was ludicrous. Had I not produced Land Registry maps, certifying my ownership of a hundred-acre lake and all contained therein, particularly the eleven-acre Heather Island, with its six-bedroomed, stone-built, slated house clearly marked thereon?

"In your own words, please tell the court the age and condition of this house you call 'home' and the circumstances in which it came into your possession." What damned impertinence! But no lizard lawman was going to get under my skin.

Heather Island and Tully Lake formed part of the Renvyle Estate, purchased by the Blake family from the Earl of Westmeath in 1668, on their return from Montserrat. One of that family built his house on Heather Island in 1860. My grandfather purchased the Blake Estate in 1917 and subsequently restored and extended the old house to its present proportions. It has come down to me through my parents. It is a perfectly splendid house, in a setting that many have called unique." That would fairly soften his cough, this irritating upstart called Mullarkey!

"Very interesting. Very, very interesting indeed. You would seem to have a strongly developed sense of history. But let me ask you about the present. Does your house have electricity?"

"No, it does not. We have always found oil lamps and candles more than sufficient to our needs where lighting is concerned. As for heat, we have numerous open fires and a stove for heating the water. Cooking is done by gas, on which the refrigerator also runs." That's the way to deal with johnnie jumped-ups.

11

"Fascinating. Though perhaps a trifle spartan to modern minds; for women and children particularly. But let that pass for the moment. You spoke of your house having been restored by your grandfather. That will have been a number of years ago now?"

"Obviously, since he died in 1957. However, it has been maintained in the meantime."

"Do you say so? Is it not the case that many of the steel windows are in a state of woeful disrepair, that the veranda is deemed unsafe and that plaster crashes from the ground floor ceilings whenever a person walks through the rooms above?" .

"There is an amount of work to be done, I admit. The house has not been continuously inhabited since the Duke of Leinster lived there during the war years." Titles command respect. .

"Are you telling the court that what you call 'home' is a semi-derelict house on an island in Connemara, unlived-in since being abandoned by a thrice-divorced, undischarged bankrupt fifty years ago? Would you have this court believe that the property so described is a safe and suitable habitat for your wife and children? I put it to you that you are acting irresponsibly, that your proposals are verging on lunacy!'

My mute appeal to the judge brought a grudging, "Out of order, Mr. Mullarkey. The court has heard enough. Judgement is reserved, pending a further report three months hence. Case adjourned."

I woke with a start, scrambling to separate dreams from reality, comforted by the familiar appearance of the crack in the plaster over the chimney flue running jaggedly from eye level to ceiling. I was safe on my island. It had all been just a bad dream, not even a nightmare. Nightmares are scary. This nonsense had only served to underline the potential mischief that modern, urbanised "society" can inflict on decent, law-abiding citizens whose circumstances and surroundings identify them as "different". That's all. Bloody busybodies. Get

up. Get going. Work to be done! The "three months" was right,
though. If I hadn't made this place habitable and accessible by
the end of September, I was in trouble ...

My gregarious, half-American wife was in no hurry to
forsake the comfort and style of friends' smart Yorkshire
houses to take on the resurrection of this "rookery", as she
called it. A week became two weeks, and then three. Where she
went, there the twins went also. Our eldest, married daughter
was engrossed in getting her restaurant open on the outskirts
of the Curragh of Kildare, where her husband runs a stud
farm. Our second girl had inveigled her way into the property
market in Hongkong, while the third was in the throes of
switching universities somewhere in the English midlands.
Even had any of the three girls been at a loose end, they knew
better than to get involved.

I wasn't tempted to invite anyone to share in my campaign
to render the "rookery" fit for continuous occupation,
conscious that, while I could stomach my own culinary
creations, others might not. I needn't have worried. Frederick
Norton Peters—more familiarly known simply as "Pete"—
announced his arrival from Yorkshire, for his annual week's
rest and recreation in Connemara; no wife, no children. And
Pete could cook! He had put me up when I had first moved to
Yorkshire to work for the Jockey Club. Pete was a bachelor in
those days, and I a sole traveller. Though now an eminently
respectable, clean-living family man, running his own,
successful car business, Pete had had other, more colourful
careers in his time and knew his way around. By strange
coincidence he had spent some time in nearby Renvyle House
Hotel years before—autre temps, autre mœurs, autre femme.
Able to turn his hand to anything, and enjoy a drink, he was a
welcome ally.

Pete's arrival conveniently coincided with my purchase of a
gleaming, petrol-driven generator from Shane Ruane,

engineer, commercial diver and racing driver. That its black and yellow livery was similar to that of a wasp didn't strike me at the time … Amazingly, Shane Ruane of Renvyle knew all about Macau, it being his dearest ambition to compete in the unofficial Formula Three world championship, staged there each autumn. Ours was almost a perverse conversation. I had thrown up a job in Macau to come and live in Renvyle. Shane, born and reared in Renvyle, saw Macau as his Mecca. Not many round here have heard of Macau, and fewer still could say where it is.

It took six of us to get the generator into the boat, out of the boat, up the path, "that winds crimson-walled by fuchsia, and roofed by laurel, rhododendron and flowering shrubs" and into the toolshed, its new home. Shane, whose back was "awful bad", had "volunteered" the services of his younger brother, Paud, the local electrician-cum-plumber. Paud rigged up the surly machine, ran a cable through the undergrowth to the battery at the foot of the telegraph pole and bade me hit the starter button.

The generator roared into life, shattering the peace and quiet of a summer's evening, and Heather Island now had an electricity supply. Breakthrough! Tired but triumphant, we repaired forthwith to the Renvyle Inn, to toast our epic achievement, not once, not twice, but until that familiar refrain was heard, "Have yez no homes to go to!"

The advent of electricity on Heather Island was to prove the greatest single "improvement" to have occurred to the old place, at least in my lifetime of summers spent there. Mains electricity would be better still, not least because it is noiseless, which our generator most definitely was not. But that was only a matter of time. My application had been acknowledged. The Electricity Supply Board's Customer Services Engineer would be calling upon me on completion of his summer holidays. In the meantime the availability of power, from whatever source, transformed the attitudes of the local artisans. They had fought shy of undertaking any but the most superficial jobs on the island for the simple reason that they couldn't utilise power tools. That the house was still completely unwired didn't matter. A series of extension leads would suffice.

Pete's return to "civilisation" presaged the arrival of Milady and the twins, to scenes and sounds of bedlam. The two Michaels had set up their portable sawmill in the "little court paved with irregular slats, russet and brown and sea-green." The condemned veranda had disappeared, leaving the four doors that opened on to it looking temporarily ridiculous, opening for the present into space. To replace it with new timbers took a week, for the veranda is all of sixty feet long and none of its floorboards or rails were salvageable. Milady was clearly disconcerted. That progress had been made was indisputable; more in three weeks than in her twenty-something summers here, as girlfriend, fiancée, wife and mother of five.

Milady's confusion was understandable. Practical—as womenfolk need to be—she had difficulty reconciling this frenzied restoration programme in a summer holiday home, that no sane person would willingly inhabit in winter, with the more pressing business of my securing a "proper job". "Connemara's lovely, in summer. But this island, in winter? Besides, we can't live on scenery. Why throw money we can't afford at a house we can't inhabit? What are we going to live on when the money's all spent? I told you you were mad when you took out a racehorse trainer's licence, and I was right. But at least that brought in some money. How do you suppose we're going to survive? I used to think you were loony. Now I know you're BARKING MAD!"

Come to think of it now, the word used may not have been "barking", but the din of the bandsaws, ripsaws and power drills may have distorted it. And there was no judge to rule

15

Milady's remarks "Out of order". As our fax machine refused to function in these primitive surroundings, strategic retreats to Renvyle House Hotel were the order of the day, in insincere pursuit of dreaded "proper jobs" in some miserable, malarial clime. Milady had been a little harsh about my training venture, seeing that her own father, "the Captain", had reared a family of eleven (of which Milady was the youngest) in a similar capacity. Her brothers had all been jockeys and trainers. One of them—the late, lamented John—had helped me to emulate my father-in-law in training an Irish Grand National winner. John had also been an ardent Heather Island devotee. His persuasive charm would have been welcome now.

Did Milady's intuition predict my continuing failure to land that "proper job"? Or was she simply proving a point? Whatever the reason, she promptly set an example to her dilatory spouse by joining the ever-swelling payroll at Kylemore Abbey, charged with organising, deflecting and diffusing coachloads of ravenous tourists. At the height of the season—in August—as many as fifty coaches pull into the spacious grounds of Kylemore Abbey each day, all in search of facilities, food and shopping.

To an operation of its considerable size, such numbers would not create any major problem, were they not all prone to arrive at more or less the same time—lunchtime. Originating, as many of them do, from as far away as Lisdoonvarna in County Clare, these coachloads arrive with keenly whetted appetites, all expecting instantaneous gratification. Moreover, their schedules are so tight that any delay causes voluble unrest among drivers and couriers alike. The tourists are easier to appease, for they are content to be told where they actually are, as opposed to where they ought to be.

Milady adores people—the more the merrier. Irrespective of colour, class or creed, they would all be greeted with a flashing smile and educated English, delivered at the speed of a Gatling gun. This fortuitous development had the same effect on the denizens of Heather Island as releasing the valve on a pressure cooker. In my unaccustomed role of "house parent" I could initiate the twins in essential aspects of Irish culture ...

The Galway Races—the greatest carnival in the Irish social calendar—take place at the end of July. The twins were enthusiastic about venturing in, preferably on the Wednesday, "Plate day". The Galway Plate is the highlight of the summer jumping season in Ireland; a prize I coveted in my time as a trainer. The Galway Races form part of our heritage and tradition, a place of pilgrimage for thousands, year in and year out. One local man still treasured the racecard from his initial visit. That was in 1904 and he hadn't missed a meeting since!

Nicholas and Camellia had become somewhat race-starved, for children are barred from racemeetings in the Far East; an admission on the authorities' behalf that racing in the Orient is just about betting. Not that this consideration was to prevent my intrepid apprentice punters from "doing their dough" in the thronged enclosures of sunny, windswept Ballybrit. High on a hill to the east of the city, Ballybrit looks out to Galway Bay and the hills of Clare beyond. The sweeping, right-handed track encompasses an old, ruined castle, reminder of other and more troublous times, when the "Citie of the Tribes", being staunchly royalist, found itself beleaguered from the west by the "ferocious O'Flaherties" and from the east by Cromwell's armies.

It was strange, renewing acquaintances of ten years past, when I was scraping a living out of realising others' dreams. Well, sometimes, anyway. "And tell us this. Where are you living now? Is it in China you are still?"

"No, no, had enough of that. I'm in Connemara now." The ultimate heresy. Everyone knew there was no racing west of Galway. Shaking heads, muttered disbelief, and another encounter ended. Racing folk are reluctant to converse on other topics, and certainly not in the hurly-burly of Ballybrit. On the way back out to Connemara it dawned on me that my decision to come and live out here meant cutting myself off from my youthful passion and adult profession.

August

━━━━━━━━━━━━━━━━━━━━━━━ ❧ ━━━━━━━━━━━━━━━━━━━━━━━

While the Galway Races mark the beginning of the traditional holiday period in Ireland, they also coincide with the first, horribly premature intimations of autumn. The linden trees that overhang the "little court paved with irregular slats, russet and brown and sea-green" are the earliest harbingers of the season of mists and mellow fruitfulness on Heather Island. The leaves at the very ends of the branches overhanging the old, upended rowing boat, that now serves as an occasional sunbed, surreptitiously turn from emerald green to palest yellow and later through golden to russet. My three-month "judgement reserved" had but two months to run ...

By now we were agreed that the twins, Nicholas and Camellia, should continue their education in Ireland, irrespective of our subsequent movements. Through a series of fortuitous developments Nicholas gained acceptance to Glenstal Abbey, outside Limerick, while Camellia was granted a place in the Ursuline Convent School, Thurles, in neighbouring County Tipperary. Lucky, once again. Cosmopolitan children, by virtue of their travels, they would find boarding school less traumatic than many of their contemporaries, raised in constant, familiar, unchanging surroundings. The twins seemed philosophical, if their mother did not. At least they were now assured of a decent education; proof against their parents' possible peregrinations.

19

The conclusion of the Galway Races seemed to signal a subliminal resumption of what passes for "normality" in Connemara. Thus were we favoured with a visit from the ESB's Customer Services Engineer, a troubled little man, whose mind appeared constantly elsewhere. His disclosures explained his demeanour ... An overhead supply would cost me Nine Thousand Pounds, including the VAT of course. An underwater supply was clearly deemed preposterous, as his quotation — Twenty-three Thousand Pounds — confirmed. Of course an overhead supply will require Planning Permission, seeing as your house is in an area of high scenic amenity. That could take three months for the County Council to decide. Then, when we get the go-ahead from them — if we do — and we get your money — in advance — we might be able to begin work within a further eight weeks. Though, mind you, we'd be well into the winter by then. It'd be nearly as well to maybe to leave it over till next year . . .

Maybe the Greeks had it right; killing the messenger who brought unwelcome tidings. But shooting would be much too good for this misbegotten emissary of that monolithic state monopoly, the ESB. And to think that the telephone "service" had been no better, until its bloated bureaucracy had been blasted away by a degree of privatisation. Compare and contrast now! In his half-hearted attempt to sugar a most unpalatable pill, the emissary muttered about the possibility of grant aid, where it could be proved that more than half an applicant's income was derived from farming. The desirability of instant acquisition of sheep was mooted. Useless to retort that a visiting journalist had recently described Ireland as: "A medium-sized island off the mainland of Europe being steadily consumed by sheep."

Stupidly, as it transpired, I spent a lot of time and energy in trying to obtain an ESB supply at any half-reasonable price, lobbying TDs and Government Ministers of whatever hue.

Questions were tabled in the Dáil, feelers extended in Brussels, a case put before the regional tourism office. Futile. Hopeless. Funding was exclusively for farmers. Never mind that insane headage payments on useless, unwanted ewes have denuded the hills of Connemara, filthying the finest salmon rivers in Europe, enriching magnificent lakes to the threatened extinction of game angling. Never mind. Pay up, and look cheerful about it, sap!

Was I tempted to abandon this madcap scheme and walk away, for nine thousand quid? I was, briefly. But then I thought of the alternatives; and pressed on in pursuit of my dream. Heather Island was to become "home", our home, come hell or high water. And they came. Oh, yes sirree. They came!

Hell and high water were still but spectres on our horizon when "Batman" struck. This personable young ranger in the wildlife department of the Connemara National Park had heard of the Heather Island bat colony and duly quizzed the twins on one of our regular evening forays to buy provisions in one end of the Letterfrack trading post, followed by "cocktails" in the other. More often than not the third section received our custom as well, supplying as it does those nuts and bolts, paints and general hardware with which to hold old houses together.

Suitably impressed by the twins' reports, the ranger made an appointment to inspect our stock of "souris volants". It just so happened that his arrival coincided with Milady's "toilette". Duly warned, Milady vacated the recently refurbished master bedroom, transferring operations to the bathroom next door. Intent upon surprising these nocturnal fliers during their daytime siesta, the ranger sped smartly up a ladder and disappeared into the attic above our bedroom. Evidence of his ascent survives in the form of a football-sized oedema in the newly plastered ceiling. Undaunted, our hero switched to external observation, shinning up the ladder and appearing suddenly outside the bathroom window. Covered in confusion,

Milady wrenched the curtains together. Sadly, the curtains failed to swish, crashing to the floor, rail and all. "Batman" as he had now become for ever more, descended in disorder, declaring his survey suspended, pending the arrival of his lady superior in matters chiropteric, aka "Batwoman". He left the twins some window stickers bearing the legend "Bats need Friends". One friend and fellow-sceptic, veteran of many Heather Island escapades, could not let this pass unremarked . . . "With friends like him they can't afford enemies!"

While all of this commotion had occurred in less time than it takes to write, it had totally disconcerted not just Milady, but "Stan the Shovel" as well. Stanley had been recommended as Heather Island's only answer to a mechanical digger, for such we really needed to excavate and expose the dyspeptic, flatulent sewage system. Installed in the 'twenties, when my grandparents had resurrected the old house, the pipes and tanks had been laid by "old Ulick" Joyce, plumber extraordinaire. He had taken the secrets of Heather Island's effluent system to his grave, neglecting to pass on this vital information to his son and successor, Bunny Joyce. Anyway, Bunny's heart wasn't in it. He preferred playing in dance bands. On the last occasion we had inveigled him into doing anything on the island he had shattered a shiny new lavatory bowl in his attempts to upgrade us in the vitreous china department. Eventually convinced that a better quality of life lay in filling bladders rather than emptying them, Bunny had forsaken plumbing and become a publican.

The demise of "old Ulick" and the disaffection of his son and heir had created a vacuum — if that is the appropriate word in this calling. It had duly been filled by Paud, Shane Ruane's younger brother. Naturally, in his dual role of plumber and electrician, Paud could not prostitute his professional standing in the community by navvying. Enter Stan the Shovel, from the slopes of Letter Hill, that "great rock", of which Gogarty wrote as sheltering heather Island from the prevailing winds. Paud had nominated Stanley, suspecting—rightly—that my amateurish attempts would leave the septic tank's whereabouts a secret for at least as long as the tomb of Tutankhamun.

Operating instructions that preceded Stanley's arrival were succinct. "Give him a shovel. Take him to the starting point. Face him in the right direction. And feck off!" Intrigued, I had welcomed this lithe, tanned man-machine with a shovel, as specified, and a step spade as well, to remove the upper crust of scraw and roots. Stanley had simply smiled at the spade, taken the shovel and set to work with the strength of a rockbreaker and the deftness of a surgeon. Drains, undisturbed for decades, so long indeed that their very existence might have been dubious, were swiftly exposed, and in their wake a series of septic tanks that could have serviced the city of Galway. Stanley had begun the final phase of his excavation—the soak pit—when Batman's antics had distracted him. Casting aside my now scalpel-sharp shovel, Stanley declared a suddenly remembered but urgent engagement ashore. The shovel was well rusted ere we saw Stanley again. However, at least we now knew where the sewage ran and thus where to investigate in those sordid circumstances when it might cease so to run ...

The summer holiday season brought its customary succession of house guests, family friends for the most part, who had been coming down to stay each summer for years, "camping indoors", as one wag had described it. In some cases their children, now grown up, had begun to return under their own steam, regaling each other with childhood memories of the island and adding aspects unseen by adult eyes. And sooner or later each and every one, in various ways, would moot the same concern. .Do you really believe you'll survive a winter on the island? The practically minded spoke of storms, while the more philosophically inclined warned of the dangers of love turning to hatred.

Mat, the pragmatist, offered us his Jotul, a state of the art wood-burning stove that he had had installed in his portion of what had once been Sir Horace Plunkett's house in Foxrock — Kilteragh Pines. During the Civil War the IRA had needed two attempts to destroy Kilteragh Pines, commencing with explosives and concluding with arson. The "expert fitter" employed to install Mat's Jotul had come close to accomplishing what the IRA could not, by the simple expedient of running the flue through a timber collar ... While conceding that the damage caused by the fire had been negligible in comparison to the carnage achieved by those enlisted to extinguish it, Mat had become disenchanted with his new toy. It was ours for the taking away.

Such a gift horse was not to have its mouth scrutinised. True, our existing boiler had served us well, over a very long number of years, cheerfully consuming everything from wet timber to tin cans. But of late it had begun to exhibit a disconcerting dependency on the prevailing wind from the south west. Asked to contend with winds from any other quarter, it swiftly created conditions in the hallway fit to kipper entire crates of herring. Paud fitted the Jotul and, that same day, the Stanley range in the kitchen. Now we were getting places, I averred. Milady remained unconvinced. What have you done about Singapore? became instead What's happening with the ESB? In truth an impasse had arisen. My pleas that half my income derived from agriculture, or could be said to, since I had no income, availed me nought . . . Besides, Paud declined to wire the house until such time as he should have, in his own words, "the run of the place."

The August Bank Holiday (British version) marks the end of the summer season in Connemara, as the lushness of the fuchsia fades, the blackberries ripen in the hedgerows and thoughts turn towards the start of another school year. This year it was, in many ways, a relief. We had accomplished a lot, albeit from a very, very basic starting point, and we still relied on paraffin lamps and candles; the more so as the evenings drew perceptibly in. Lamps and candles create an atmosphere, late of a summer's evening, attracting as they do all manner of moths and fireflies. To smokers they are perhaps not inconvenient. Smokers invariably carry matches or a lighter. "Batwoman" professed herself enchanted.

Yes, "Batman" did return, this time as assistant, guide and general protector to "Batwoman". Kate—for that her name was—had responsibility for the welfare of the bat population from Cork to Donegal. As we were more or less halfway she was particularly interested to identify which of the seven indigenous species inhabited Heather Island. The twins could hardly contain their excitement, though in Camellia's case there was an added element of guilt. Growing tired of being dive-bombed in her bedroom one evening, she had made a grab at one as it swooped around her head, inadvertently ripping off one wing. Like a sycamore's shedding seed pod, the stricken creature had fluttered the length of the veranda to our bedroom, where it expired.

Waiting until near darkness, Kate, her acolyte and the twins, carrying the ultra-sonic equipment with which both to identify the type and record their numbers, slipped out into the gloom and took up position below the principal bat passage. This is simply a piece of old cast iron drainpipe which I had inserted in an attic gable to replace a window that had no function, other than to achieve a superfluous symmetry of design. What with nine external doors and twenty-one windows, the old house suffers from an excess of apertures. From Batman's leaflets we had learned that only Whiskered or Lesser Horseshoe bats would confer any serious "cachet". Pipistrelle would be a social disgrace, while Leisler's, Long-eared or Daubenton's would be only barely fit for mention in public (houses). Betting on the outcome was ruled to be in bad taste, as we sat around the circular, oak diningroom table in candlelight and awaited developments.

The outcome was better than the pessimists among our company predicted, while not quite realising the hopes of those convinced that only truly exotic species could inhabit Heather Island. Ours were Natterer's bats, present in sufficient numbers to make this the second largest colony of Natterer's in Connacht. As Natterer's are classified as "reasonably common", as distinct from "common", or—worst of all—"very common", we could feel pleased. So we did, toasting the health of all one hundred and sixty of our furry little fliers, until Nicholas rowed Batman and Batwoman back across the moonlit lake to their earthbound Batmobile.

That the imminent departure of the twins constituted an affront to Milady had become public knowledge; one of those moneyed affronts that the fundamentally affluent seem able to acknowledge, with grimaces and the occasional expressive shrug of inherited responsibilities. To me—a mere pawn in this greater order of things—their leaving was calamitous. We had just embarked on an eel fishing experiment. This involved shooting eel nets along strategic "runs" in Tully Lake, positioned to entrap migratory shoals of silvering eels on their eternal pilgrimage to the Sargasso Sea. Easy enough to shoot, these nets were back-breaking to lift, empty, re-align and re-shoot, in strings of seven.

The eel fishing experiment had been an unstated success. Nicholas and I had filled holding bags full of these slithery, gawping, political creatures, pending their expropriation, in aerated mobile tanks, to low-lying countries, where such are accounted staples of everyday existence. The understatement of our success may have had to do with the capture of a drowned mallard, discovered by Nicholas, on our final retrieve, upright, traumatised and totally suffocated in the final chamber of one of these fiendishly contrived serial nets. We also caught a number of decent brown trout, which no longer seemed possible by more conventional means. The fly fishing properties of Tully Lake had declined drastically over recent summers, suggesting a need to re-stock. Long gone were the days when I could slip out for an hour or so, confident of catching sufficient trout to provide dinner for the household, using three tried and trusted flies — Connemara Black, Bloody Butcher and Claret 'n Mallard.

Initiated into the art of fly fishing by my father — at considerable risk to his own safety, scourged by flailing hooks — I had fished Tully Lake avidly throughout the 'sixties, 'seventies and well into the 'eighties. Our guests had all fished too, as the fishing diaries testify. When fishing well, given the right combination of cloud, wind and wave, Tully Lake used to average a fish every ten minutes. But in recent years, the rods, though mounted and hung in readiness beneath the veranda, were rarely disturbed. The explanation for this dramatic decline in interest was simple. We were no longer catching fish. Though they were still numerous — as the eel nets proved — they were no longer surface feeding. Not that this phenomenon was peculiar to Tully Lake. Corrib, Conn and Mask had also ceased to yield the sport for which they were renowned worldwide. What had gone wrong?

Mention fish in any pub around these parts and the hum of conversation suddenly drops. Those painted signs in Oughterard and elsewhere exhorted all and sundry to "SAVE OUR SEATROUT" and "NO TO FINNED FISH FARMING". An ominous hush descended when I queried Stuart Feakes … Stuart was a fanatical Waltonian, his tweed hat and jacket lodging more flies than a porcupine sports quills. Throughout the season Stuart's rod would be clamped to the roof of his car, a familiar sight outside the pubs of Connemara. Intellectual to his fingertips, this loquacious little fish-killer had an original theory. Simple. The hole in the ozone layer. "Ultra-violet. Fish can't tolerate the rays. Don't you understand? Doesn't anybody around here understand anything?" The entire pub had now fallen silent. This could be good. Would Stuart rise a row, maybe even get barred, again?

With his jockey's physique, piercing eyes and rasping voice, Stuart had missed his vocation. He should have been an actor, for no one appreciated an audience more. And he had one now. Stuart in full flight was as good as a play, as I was about to find out, in my unwanted role as his stooge . . . "I know you not, good sir! But if you own Tully Lake, as you say, then you should realise why you no longer catch trout from it. Why, not even I consider it worth poaching any more!" I could sense the smirks. Poaching was a way of life in Connemara and Stuart had been around these parts long enough to prove his sporting prowess.

"Socialism has destroyed Tully Lake! Before this God-awful welfare state gave all these peasants fridges the earth was protected by the ozone layer. Now Connemara's crawling with skin cancer. They're all going around like Muslim women. Look at them!" Aware of the mutterings he had caused, Stuart altered tack. "The destruction of the ozone layer has affected fishing as well. Fish cannot tolerate ultra-violet rays. These remove the natural slime that every fish needs for survival. To avoid exposure to these rays the fish have to stay down deep. They have become bottom-feeders, as they daren't come to the surface to feed on fly life. That's why you're not catching them. And don't think it's just your piddling little lake. The Corrib's frigged. Mask is abandoned. Inagh the same! But who cares? They've all got fridges, full of filthy frozen foods ..."

The landlord intervened, (he sells lots of frozen foods). "That's enough now Stuart. We all know how much you know, and, indeed, how little any of the rest of us know. Let this poor man enjoy his pint in peace. For otherwise ..." Stuart—only recently reinstated in this, one of his favoured watering-holes—needed no further bidding.

Some time later—the normal hubbub restored—Batman murmured out the corner of his mouth that the more conventional explanation for the decline of fly fishing was eutrophication. Suitably impressed, I asked for a translation, in layman's terms. Eutrophication, Batman explained, was the technical term for enrichment of the lakebed in nutrients. This promoted plant growth and consequently greater bottom feeding for the trout. It would eventually kill off the trout population by depriving the fish of oxygen. This phenomenon was attributable to over-grazing of the surrounding hillsides, now intensively fertilised to support unsustainable numbers of sheep. "So, sheep farming is killing my fishing?" "It is you who have said it."

Whatever the truth might be behind the decline of our fly fishing fortunes, it would have to take its place in the order of things. In any case, the season ends on lakes in this locality in mid-September. Any serious survey would not start before next April, and such necessitated an application to the Western Regional Fisheries Board. Meanwhile, the impasse with the ESB meant that I was daily losing ground ...

Among the options mooted, discussed, discarded and resurrected for getting a living out of Heather Island, the most obvious was tourism, whether as a "Hidden House", offering accommodation, or as an "Historic House", open to the public for three months each year. We opted to explore the latter, on the basis of Heather Island being the only one of Oliver St John Gogarty's many houses still in private hands; family hands at that. Moreover, of the members of the Irish literary renaissance, Gogarty was possibly unique. He didn't have a Society dedicated to the perpetuation of his literary reputation. Enter Rupert, man of letters, lifelong friend and mendicant lecturer, known in academic circles as Melmoth the Wanderer.

"I'll round up the usual suspects. You draft the leaflet ..."

Rupert had chosen the easy part, for capturing this poet, prose writer, patriot, senator, surgeon, athlete, aviator and mordant wit is no easy task. This may be why Gogarty had remained so long marginalised in the Irish literary reincarnation that had spawned talking shops at every crossroads in the country. He defies definition. "Buck Mulligan" in Ulysses, the troubled priest in The Lake, "one of the great lyric poets of our age" in Yeats's introduction to the Oxford Book of Modern Verse and "the wittiest man in London" according to Asquith, Oliver Gogarty enjoyed many personae.

Paper never refused ink. Duly was the Gogarty Society launched, in the Shelbourne Rooms, where once upon a time he had conducted his medical practice. The launch coincided with the re-publication of Gogarty's most famous—or infamous—book, 'As I was going down Sackville Street'. The Society's first scheduled gathering would take place in Renvyle House Hotel, his former country home, in October; over the weekend that marks the end of Summer Time. As the "headquarters" of the Society, Heather Island might now expect to be favourably regarded by those responsible for the promotion of Ireland's literary trail.

One of the first responses to our new venture came from faraway Ontario. "Of course you know that Heather Island has its own history that considerably pre-dates Gogarty. My grandmother was married from Heather Island in 1897." Here was a story! Everyone knew of the Blakes—one of the fourteen founding "tribes" of Galway—and of the return of one Henry Blake from Montserrat to purchase the Renvyle Estate in the 17th century. His descendants had only given up the unequal struggle in 1917, selling out to my forebear. But this bride from Heather Island, how did she fit in?

Athelstane Blake, one of seven sons of Henry Blake of Renvyle, had built the original house on Heather Island around 1860. Six years later he had wooed and wed Sophia

Marguerite Gaudard from Lausanne, a niece of one of the co-founders of the Red Cross, and installed his new bride as chatelaine of Heather Island. And Milady found her predicament peculiar! Their daughter, Ellen Marguerite — already known as "the lady of the lake" — had married a Dublin doctor and borne him five daughters. Their children, in turn, had married and dispersed all over the globe; thus this intriguing snippet of history from overseas.

My Canadian informant made no reference to the local legend which held that Athelstane Blake had used the stone from a pre-historic crannóg at the eastern end of the lake as building material for his Heather Island house. However, that information was recorded in an archaeological survey of the Renvyle area in the 1880s and there seems no good reason to doubt it. Gogarty made reference to this in "Freilaun" ... "Yes; south of Half-Moon Island is a round island not much larger than a tennis-court. It was once surrounded by large stones which were removed when old Blake, the Sunday man, built a cottage on Freilaun. A Sunday man is not necessarily a devotee, but one who could move freely only on Sundays, for on that day the King's Writ did not run; and debtors were safe. Blake removed the encircling stones and with them traces of one of the oldest of habitations — a dwelling on a crannóg or island (usually artificial) in lake or marsh. These may be compared to the pile-dwellings in the lakes of Switzerland.

"Why men wished to crowd on an island little bigger than a large room is hard to say. It may have been to keep their children safe from the wolves that were a pest that could not be exterminated. Whatever compelled them who can tell. But that they lived on a crannóg in Tully Lake is indisputable; their bone needles were found there, and what else who knows?"

Setting his piece on "Freilaun" in the height of a Connemara summer, Gogarty felt free to write, " There is light enough in June to go to bed without a candle; but a candle should be lit

31

to bring back a forgotten light that is softer than electric light under the mellowest of shades ... It is more soothing than electric light and easier on the eyes. It is astonishing how much light a candle can give. It is not enough for modern eyes to read by, though the greatest works in the world were written by it; but it fills the bedroom with a soporific glow."

What holds true in June is no longer valid at the end of August, when the first of the linden leaves have begun to accumulate in the courtyard and the lawn seems somehow cowed by the blazing orange ranks of waving montbretia that now surround it. The atmosphere grows thinner; as can be seen by the ease with which the plunger in the cafetière may now be depressed. The morning sunshine no longer warms the east-facing kitchen for as long. The time had come to treat with the ESB. I could hold out, in the hopes of getting a grant by some obscure means ... My reading of the runes indicated an appointment with one of those high street financial institutions, now unashamedly boasting profits in excess of one million pounds per day.

That the bank manager—even out in Clifden—should turn out to be a racing man did not come as a complete surprise. Many of them admit to this form of escapism from their slide-rule existence. While I never trained a horse for a bank official per se, it was occasionally brought to my notice that an alarming number of the quadrupeds in my care appeared to have no other sponsor. Pleasant to be rid of such preoccupations. Curiously, confirmation of the bank manager's willingness to underwrite the electrification of Heather Island signalled an end to any further mention of planning permission. Work could commence within weeks. The twins were intrigued. Did this mean that we could enjoy such basic features of civilisation as TV? And how long might it take? And would everything be up and running by the time of their first weekend home from their respective academies? And did this mean that we could now bring over the contents of our erstwhile "home" in Yorkshire?

Well, we'd see. One thing at a time. But I knew what they meant. Their entire childhood was stored in two twenty-foot containers in a warehouse somewhere in Leeds; possessions unseen since their departure to Macau, what seemed like ages and ages ago. A week can appear an infinity at twelve, in Connemara, when all your summer friends have returned to their comfortable houses where everything works, and you are facing the unknowns of boarding school.

The twins' departure to points south and slightly more southeast was immediately prefaced by the arrival of the ESB poles, and the departure of the eels. Vast piles of dark brown poles mysteriously appeared on the side of our "avenue", evidence at least of intent. Excitement mounted. It really was going to happen, after all! Then the eel men arrived, with their aerated tanks bubbling away on the back of a truck. Nicholas had mentally spent his share ten times over. The cumbersome nets—so awkward to handle on dry land—were stowed. It was time to pull in the holding bags from their anchorage in the lee of Heather Island. These were of much heavier construction than the catching nets, with ropes thick enough to thwart the otters that silently share the island with us. The first one hauled ashore was very heavy indeed, full of the finest of silvering eels. The Dutchman was ecstatic, "Zees are verra goot, verra goot." The second bag seemed to follow the boat too readily, with nothing like the same resistance. The Dutchman was visibly disappointed. Diligent examination duly found the hole, just big enough for the smaller eels to have escaped through. They had gone, and with them a substantial proportion of our anticipated reward. But never mind. It was money earned from the waters of Tully Lake that we would not otherwise have had and proof that there would always be a few quid to be got from that source in the years to come, if times got bad.

Finally—and in some ways symbolically—as the first summer of permanent occupation drew to its close, the twins brought home a cat. it had followed them down the avenue, mewing for their company and apparently undeterred by the water. They had been plainly disconcerted when Milady had pointed out that it must belong to one of the houses on the hillsides surrounding the lake and would therefore have to be brought back across the lake, as it would hardly swim home. Reluctantly they had rowed it ashore and turned it loose. As it was there the following morning, and the morning after, crying to be ferried to the island once more, Milady relented. They say that you find your dog, but your cat finds you. Thus did our first "dependant" inhabit Heather Island: black and white and anonymous.

The departure of the twins, in the wake of the tourist exodus, gave us the chance to reflect on our situation. It occurred to us that we had really learned nothing of our adoptive milieu throughout all our summers spent in Connemara as holidaymakers, surrounded by similarly minded seekers after "craic agus ceol". Yes, we were aware, through Michael Viney's prophecies in *The Irish Times*, that Connemara was being denuded by over-grazing and that fish farming was a bone of contention between conservationists and those who benefited from the employment fish farming provided in the area. We knew too that the SOS (Save Our Seatrout) lobby blamed salmon farming for the disappearance of said seatrout from once-famous lakes and rivers in the region—Delphi, Erriff, Kylemore, Ballynahinch and Cashel. They had appealed to the government to intervene.

What we had not realised, absorbed in having "a good time", was the depth of feeling that seethed just below the surface of an ostensibly tourist-orientated community. Supporters of angling resented the profitable plunder of the netsmen, while both camps detested the perceived effects of the fish farmers' cages in the bays around this indented coastline. The fish farmers, for their part, blamed over-grazing for all the environmental damage. And everybody knew everybody else's business. We had been swimming on the surface of very murky waters, in headlong, hedonistic pursuit of pleasure. Would it be possible to live and socialise in Connemara without becoming ourselves embroiled?

> When the landfolk of Galway converse with a stranger,
> Softly the men speak, more softly the women;
> Yet older than harp-playing, older than welcomes,
> An undertone threatens *Fomorian danger,
> When the landfolk of Galway converse with a stranger.
> "Undertone" — W. B. Stanford

Not yet accorded "resident" status in the locality — if indeed we ever would be — we should simply have to tread warily. For the present the fish farmers, blow-ins like ourselves, seemed outwardly the most welcoming to newcomers to the Connemara circle.

---

* Fomors, the sea-giants of Gaelic mythology. They are represented as more ancient than the gods (Tuatha Dé Danann), and as having been ousted by them and destroyed at the battle of Moytura.

September

Two months gone and one to go … Could I satisfy his lordship that Heather Island constituted a fit "home" for Milady and her offspring? Perhaps more to the point, could Milady herself be so persuaded? The very presence of the ESB poles on the side of the avenue seemed to provide reassurance on that score, while our uninvited cat swiftly set about proving its worth in another crucial field — rodent elimination.

That these large brown water rats wintered throughout the empty house in previous years we well knew. Anywhere an internal door had been inadvertently left closed on our departure, they had simply gnawed their way through it, leaving their calling cards liberally, both upstairs and down. While it would be optimistic to render all nine acres rat free, to keep them at a reasonable remove from the old house seemed feasible.

The black and white cat soon laid claim to the house and surrounds, marking out her territory, silent and deadly. The first casualties were the family that lived under the kitchen wall, in a recess behind the cast iron drainpipe. This we were able to establish from the series of corpses produced for our appreciation at the kitchen door, coupled with the sudden disappearance of bright eyes and whiskers surveying the lie of the land from behind the shoe of the drain pipe. If all our problems could be so smoothly resolved.

True to his word, Paud returned, guaranteed now "the run of the place", as Milady cycled the four miles to Kylemore and back each day. In the relative cool of autumn she could alternatively swish or pant across the hills and valleys of Greenmount, where Gugliemo Marconi, the Irish-Italian pioneer of wireless telegraphy, briefly sited his second Transatlantic receiving station in 1913. The remains are still to be seen in the foothills above the winding road. Having assembled his boatloads of cable and wire, fixtures and fittings, power tools and miles of extensions, Paud proceeded to show what he had meant by "the run of the place". Floorboards were wrenched, screeching, from their tongued-and-grooved tranquillity. Cable snaked through doors, windows, holes in ceilings and anywhere else that it could be forced to snake.

As a concession to the "historic house" image we had opted to do without overhead lighting, which seemed as well in view of the carnage that "sockets only" had brought about. My contribution was confined to operating the generator as and when required and otherwise producing tea for Paud and his silent apprentice. We afterwards learned the reason for the silence. The young lad was petrified of his surroundings. Totally unfounded, of course. More irrationally still, the boy would not set foot inside the master bedroom, sullenly proffering his mentor tools and materials from the bedroom door as demanded. The wiring took a fortnight to complete, thus neatly coinciding with the first appearance of the ESB crew.

The peace and quiet of the autumn shoreline was suddenly shattered by a blaze of brilliant yellow vans and trucks, dune buggies, tractors and a JCB. There were men in yellow plastic hats scurrying to and fro on the landscape. But one was in the lake, up to his armpits. What could be going on? Grounds for a Stewards' enquiry ...

"Well lads. You've got a grand day for it, though it's gone

late enough for swimming." The ganger laughed at this approach.

"You wouldn't want to mind Popeye. He's only pickin' a path across the lake for the JCB and he's well used to water — Liffey water, mainly."

"Oh, right. What depth can the JCB manage?"

"She's fairly handy that way. Up to four feet, anyhow."

"But this lake drops to twenty feet round this part, thirty in others!" There had been men drowned here in times past. Paud's uncle had been one, falling through the ice trying to rescue a sheep.

"Be the Lord God. John, come back outa that. This man says there's forty foot of water beyont!"

John's grudging return to safety, and a towel, averted one potential disaster. But it provoked a crisis …How, in the name of all that's holy, could one pole be erected on the island without the JCB? Never mind three! All activity ceased abruptly. The landscape fell still, silent, as the enormity of this unforeseen calamity hit the workforce. Three poles. Three holes. No JCB. Impossible!

Over the ensuing days, as Tommy Joyce's adjoining fields sprouted a sparse, brutal forest of dark, stark poles, it seemed to me that another form of poll had taken place — a straw poll. Sure enough, as the mainland programme reached its close, the identity of the "condemned" emerged. "Popeye" and two young riggers had been selected to take on the unthinkable — manually. Two pristine crowbars were supplied; a far, far cry from the modern machinery on which they had come to depend.

The three poles were shoved into the lake, for me to nudge over to the island with the boat. I then rowed my "condemned" crew across — and left them to it, waist-high in heather and bracken. On-site hours — never very many in any case — condensed to three per day. Miraculously, all three poles became upstanding, each one securely braced against the coming winter gales that so frequently plunged the peninsula into darkness. The heavy cables were strung with an impressive mixture of strength and technique. All that remained to achieve "service" was a trench from the final pole to the meter—my responsibility, for the ESB do not dig trenches—and "the cert" from Paud, indemnifying the ESB against electrocuting their newest customers. It sounded so simple ... even if it did necessitate the recapture of Stan the Shovel for the trenching and Paud for "the cert".

Having saved and drawn home his winter's supply of turf from the bog, Stanley was all business. Once again spurning my offer of a spade, Stan scythed a trench through scraw and sod, rocks and roots, shale and daub; the rusted spade gleaming once again as it flashed in the autumn sunlight. We now had a mains supply laid into the house.

Only "the cert" remained between us and the creature comfort of power at the flick of a switch. We could hardly wait to be freed from the increasing tyranny of the generator, which seemed to require all-too-many sick calls on Shane Ruane's part, accompanied each time by his huge, long-haired golden retriever, "Max".

It was almost certainly those visitations of "Max" that served to remind Milady of our doglessness ... "Why haven't we got a dog? We've always had dogs, even if you never liked Ruthie!" Milady was right, again. Not on one count, but on two. So we acquired two pedigree bitch pups, to be the property and putative source of revenue of the twins. "Plover", the ungainly black butter-ball of a labrador with huge paws, became Camellia's trundling treasure. "Teal", the English springer spaniel, is less easy to describe. Blue-black, shading through patches, mottled and dappled, to palest grey, she at first appeared hyper-active, nervous, almost deranged, permanently wet and shivering, physically unprepossessing.

Whatever our misgivings about a breed we had never dealt with before, they were banished by the immediate and quite remarkable "bonding" that occurred between Nicholas and herself.

They say that every man is destined to have one outstanding dog in his lifetime. Mine had been a black labrador named "Nero". That was years ago, when the older girls were small. He would lie under their pram and, as they grew older and thus mobile, act as escort and protector. In his other role Nero had been the most complete gundog any roughshooting man could wish for, equally willing to beat and retrieve in the densest and most impenetrable cover. His day's work done, Nero would lie peacefully in front of the fire in whichever hostelry claimed our custom until it was time to go home. Dignified to the last, even though ailing, Nero had bidden me a mute farewell one day, forestalling any intervention on what we both knew was his first and last leavetaking, for he had never ever strayed. No trace of our widely known and well-liked labrador was ever reported. We'd had dogs ever since — except, of course, in Macau, where dog is a delicacy — but only pale imitations of Nero. Watching Nicholas and Teal I felt that my son might have found his "Nero".

The arrival of the pups seemed to mark yet another stage in the transition of Heather Island from "house" to "home", in this, the season of "mists and mellow fruitfulness". And fruit suggested jam-making. We gathered buckets of rowans from the ring of rowan, or mountain ash, that circle the middle section of the island. They had been planted thus to ward off the bad fairies, with mixed success. The orchard yielded similar bucketfuls of apples fit only for jams or jellies and these we boiled and strained with blackberries. Milady then imported the Kylemore Abbey culinary division and, over a series of kitchen suppers and copious infusions of claret, an extraordinary array of pots of all shapes and sizes came to contain what looked like a lifetime's supply of apple jelly, blackberry 'n apple jelly and rowan jelly. While it wasn't quite "living off the land", it was a beginning. From little acorns …

Those "acorns", Milady averred, would not "get the Christmas", as they say. What could, on the other hand, contribute materially in that respect might perhaps be the completion and publication of my long-dormant manuscript on the Irish Grand National. "Had you thought about that or has this 'idyllic' existence of yours down here obliterated all thoughts of WORK?" The dreaded W-word again! How had I been so indiscreet as to mention that my co-author of long ago had resurrected that forgotten opus and secured the obvious sponsor, subject to my completing the manuscript deadline that any sane scrivener would instantly dismiss as quite simply unachievable; even with the aid of a computer and someone who knew how to operate it and, besides, until we had the ESB connected that was another non-starter and a hundred and one other excuses why "taking my eye off the ball" could prove dangerously counter-productive …

A (married) man needs to know when he's beaten. No use winning the battle, only to lose the war. An item in the paper provided the vital clue. One Alan Harman had a piece in *The Irish Times* — no less — about his landlady putting up a monument in the nearby graveyard for unbaptised babies and having the graveyard blessed and consecrated. His style suggested experience in journalism, and, perhaps, computers. Bernice, forbidding but kindhearted custodian of the local shop, marked my card. "Sure, of course you know that man. He's the one who buys all the papers every day. God only knows why! You'll find him below in Mary Sammon's cottage. And if he's not there it's only because he's in the pub, giving out about Ireland bein' a Third World country!"

"God be with the days when the likes of him were run out of it! Now it's them feckin' fish farms … pollutin' the place with their friggin' cages." This from a disembodied voice somewhere behind me.

But "them feckin' fish farms" were none of my concern. Not now anyway. I had seen this Hemingway lookalike collecting his bales of newspapers, glowered at by Bernice as he rolled out to his battered little Ford, long since bereft of silencers and shock absorbers; a true Connemara car. "Hemingway" belied his reputation. "Why not. Jest get your ass down here. There's the computer. Here's a disk. Now what you say to a beer?" Well, it would never happen in England! For much of that month of Indian summer I sat in front of this bearded Kiwi's nicotine-coated keyboard and bashed out the balance of my long-neglected manuscript, while "Hemingway" clipped items from his ever-growing piles of newspapers, watched what he called "stories breaking" on Sky News, rewrote them "Toronto-style" and sent them to potential media customers worldwide via E-mail and the Internet. It was a revelation.

Barred from Renvyle House for once too often discoursing to all and sundry on his favourite topic — Ireland and its Third World status — "Hemingway" consoled himself nightly with a bottle of Paddy and spent his days disseminating secondhand news all over the globe, from a cottage overlooking the Atlantic, in the last parish before New York. A good-natured life's traveller, "Hemingway" gave me his life history, while organising my screeds of text into a format fit to send to the waiting printers. As one used to getting paid for each word or line reproduced in Canada, Chile or China, "Hemingway" was dubious of the effort-to-reward ratio "of a whole god-damn book on horses." But he got me through it, and in time. A decent scout, "Hemingway".

Happily engrossed during working hours, while Milady administered her coachloads in the fairytale setting of Kylemore Abbey, I was reminded each evening of our primitive dependence on the sulky generator, pending Paud's crucial "cert". Paud was proving evasive, bolting when surprised in the pub, pleading horrendous pressure of work. "Sure I know well it'd take no time at all. But, be the Lord Jaysus, I'm making prisoners of minutes. 'Tis the same every Christmas with these women round here!" Surely I had misheard, hadn't I? Or was this an instance of a Galway landsman speaking softly to a stranger? While the generator constituted that "Fomorian danger".

Likewise, Shane Ruane had become disenchanted with all-too-frequent distress calls from Heather Island. His time was better spent diving to rid the fish farm cages of dead salmon, not to mention his mussel farming operation in the Killary. Eventually he resorted to prescribing various tricks of the trade, over the 'phone, when that instrument worked. None of them proved lastingly effective. Until, one rainy day, he came up with this ingenious ruse. "Do you know what you'll do ..." My spirits sank, for I have never managed to develop any affinity for infernal combustion engines. "Take out the plug, and pour a quarter cup of petrol straight into the cylinder. Only a quarter cup mind! Put back the plug and give her a dart." Dubious, and not a little afraid, I did as directed, gingerly. Eureka! The obstinate brute roared to life, reviving the dying 'phone in the process. A "retired" wine glass was immediately set aside for what was to become an ongoing ritual, until Paud should produce that vital "cert".

This wonderful Indian summer opened with the Clifden Jazz Festival and closed with the Clifden Arts Week, both events intended to extend the tourism season in the "capital of Connemara". In between we received our first warning of what the winter could bring ... Invited to lunch one day by friends waiting to sail their yacht back into Galway at the end of the season, we had got halfway across the lake when I became afraid that our unstable little boat was going to capsize if we encountered the rollers sweeping down the middle of our

43

passage. Milady is not a strong swimmer and lunch hardly seemed worth swimming for in any case. We turned tail and rowed for the lee of the island. It was a caution. A better boat would have to be found, not to mention lifejackets for all.

An autumn visit from Mat Farrelly seemed a propitious excuse to take a trip to Cong, that fishing village between Corrib and Mask, where boats abound, many for sale at the end of each season. Our journey took us along the Killary fiord with its many mussel farms, through Leenane, where John B. Keane's famous play, *The Field* had been made into a compelling film, starring Richard Harris, thereby bringing a tourist boom to this little hamlet at the head of the Killary.

The road wends its way through the Maam valley, then up alongside the western shores of Loch Corrib, that inland sea, and eventually to Cong, of the Celtic cross, ruined abbey and exclusive Ashford Castle. Designed for far bigger expanses of water that Tully Lake, none of the boats on offer proved appropriate. Besides, the era of propulsion by oars alone is old hat on the larger western lakes, whereas an engine on Tully Lake, particularly in winter conditions, could all too easily lead to disaster. Strategic outcrops of rock leave too slender a margin of error on the passage from island to shore. The answer lay at the other end of Loch Corrib, where a craftsman still made elegant larch and oak lake boats. He promised to have one ready by Christmas. That would have to do.

In the meantime turf must be laid in, and from a third party, as Heather Island's turbiary rights on the mainland had been exhausted decades since. Turf, it transpired, was sold in trailerloads; an imprecise measure, for no two trailers appeared of similar size. After many broken promises a supplier finally came to the fore, his venerable Ford Dexter lurching down our pitted avenue with a creeled tipping trailer swaying crazily in its wake. The accompanying cast of three, in a performance that would have been acclaimed in the Abbey Theatre, eventually succeeded in spewing most of their load into the boathouse, leaving its repositioning to ourselves. The rickety trailer contained an impressive amount of sods, by the time these had been thrown from the doorway into a more convenient recess within. Getting supplies across to the island would involve the repeated filling of fertiliser bags as the need arose and the weather permitted. Once again I began to wonder; not about the quality of life, but its price in hardship terms.

Michael Gibbons, Connemara's indigenous and irrepressibly enthusiastic historian and archaeologist, had no such doubts. This engaging guide and mentor to intrepid tourists had earlier led a hill-walking expedition over Letter Hill, "the great rock which shelters Tully Lake from the prevailing winds". Filmed by RTE, Michael's expedition had been shown on television just days before we met and taped by Bernice for our appreciation. I could see what they both meant. The shots of Heather Island and Tully lake from the slopes of Letter Hill made it appear the most romantic spot on earth, a sanctuary beyond price.

Michael had, that very day, led a "dig" on nearby Omey Island, accessible from the village of Claddaghduff at low tide. From his pocket he produced a Spanish silver coin that he had unearthed. Dated 1588, it bore mute testimony to the legend of a Spanish warship being wrecked off Omey during the Armada's disastrous retreat down this perilous Atlantic coast. How had it evaded discovery over the intervening four centuries? Perhaps it had been discovered, only to be reinterred through fear of death at the hands of Bingham's forces for aiding and abetting the shipwrecked Spanish soldiers. Just one more of the endless enigmas that constitute the history of Connemara, the last great wilderness in Europe.

Despite a schedule of field work and tours that sounded daunting, Michael agreed to address the Gogarty Society on his recent discoveries that would cause the history of Croagh Patrick to be rewritten. My grandfather's second prose work was entitled *I Follow Saint Patrick*, an odyssey that had taken him to the summit of Ireland's sacred mountain, directly across the bay to the north of here.

Meanwhile, arrangements for the Gogarty Society's "convention" in Renvyle House, his former country home, were taking shape, encouraged by an enthusiastic response from an eclectic array of founder members, some recruited during a reconnaissance mission to the Oscar Wilde Weekend, held in Bray at the beginning of the month. We began to pray for fine weather for our October weekend. That would mean the difference between success and failure, in Connemara, at that time of year. Another of Gogarty's books he had entitled *It isn't this time of year at all!* We Irish are said to be obsessed by the weather. It opens every conversation. Living on an island makes one acutely aware of weather conditions, actual and forecast. Over the coming winter the weather would dictate our lives, determining our freedom to come and go.

This Indian summer with its literary focus was rudely interrupted by the arrival of a forty-page application form from the Central Fisheries Board, to be completed in every detail and submitted forthwith, to qualify for possible EU funding. Pint-oiled reminiscences of seatrout in Tully Lake of old would not serve. Figures were all; numbers to be employed, tourists to be attracted, by month and even nationality. It was mind-boggling and definitely in the category of problems (to be) shared, and thereby halved. Malcolm, one of our new-found fish farming friends, was keenly interested in a pilot project to determine the viability of re-introducing a run of seatrout into Tully Lake.

His concept—based on Scandinavian methods—involved stocking the lower reaches of the stream leading down to the sea with smolts. By denying them access to the lake, he planned to force them seawards and monitor their weight gain on their eventual return. By progressively moving the barrier upstream and ultimately removing it altogether, he hoped to re-introduce a strain of sea-going trout, as had existed in Tully Lake fifty years before. Then the overall level of the lake had been higher and stocks of natural feeding lower. Eutrophication of western lakes was unknown in those days. Malcolm made it all sound beguilingly straightforward; plain common sense. But he was a fish farmer, albeit an ex-fish farmer, and branded locally for all time as a fish farmer. Had he not pioneered salmon cages in North Connemara? It seemed prudent to seek a second opinion.

Across the Killary lies the renowned Delphi fishery system, owned by Peter Mantle, an enthusiastic and determined Englishman, who had sunk all that he could afford, and considerably more besides, into resurrecting this ailing system. As one of the hardest hit by the collapse of the traditional sea trout runs, Peter had emerged as the spokesman for SOS. His advice, while freely imparted, was decidedly enigmatic. "Jolly good idea! By all means give it a try. Count yourself fortunate if it fails!" This from an Englishman? Surely some mistake here ...

Peter wasn't being entirely abstruse, as he went on to explain. "Sea trout, you must understand, are simply brown trout driven to sea by hunger. If your brownies are not going to sea it's because they have sufficient feed for their needs in your lake. Besides, good brown trout fishing is becoming increasingly sought after, particularly now that sea trout numbers have fallen to nothing. If you do manage to introduce sea-going fish, it will only be at the expense of your brownie fishing. Of course, it's up to you!"

Oh God. Why is nothing ever straightforward, least of all in Connemara? We might as well submit the application. It would be six months anyway before the next move. In went the figures for net barriers, traps, gravel and earthworks, pan-jetting and river clearance, accompanied by registered maps and proof of title. Faint hearts ne'er won EU funding. Diplomacy dictated mentioning my ideas to the Culfin Anglers Club, in the person of Malachy Kane, fanatical fisherman, sometime builder. We would meet, appropriately, in the Anglers' Rest, in nearby Tullycross, overlooking Tully Lake. Pubs provide the business and social fulcrum of life in Connemara, particularly during the off-season, when such resources revert to the resident population.

Malachy's wild-eyed, startled appearance was offset by that of his silver-haired, stocky accomplice, Phelim O'Flaherty, a fellow-officer of the Culfin Anglers, formed some years ago to transmit the members' love of fly fishing to the youth of the parish. Their efforts deserved every encouragement, for success would eventually bring to an end the age-old scourge of otter boards, or claw-lining as they call it around these parts.

Otter boards—so named because of their deadly effectiveness in depleting trout stocks—are flat pieces of timber the size of a slim briefcase and weighted with a bar of lead on the outer edge which ensures that they drift outwards from the shore, carrying in their wake a line festooned with fishing flies. As the operator walks slowly along the water's edge, so does the otter board keep pace parallel. Besides catching many trout, this illegal apparatus tears and damages huge numbers of fish. Those that recover will never again feed on the surface. Thus, from an angling point of view, they might as well no longer exist. The otter board tradition, entrenched in the Renvyle area until recent times, has begun to wane, thanks primarily to the example and encouragement offered by the Culfin Anglers. These same sportsmen were not above speaking in "soft tones" to their own as they might to strangers.

Following the customary dissection of the recent weather and how the runes read for the forthcoming winter, Phelim ventured that the collapse of sea trout stocks "would draw a tear from a boiled egg." Not, perhaps, how Peter Mantle would have put it, but expressive nonetheless! The lads seemed in favour of my proposed experiment, tacitly aware that vigilance would be required to ensure it of a reasonable chance of success. Enough said.

The conversation turned to shooting and the prospects for the season that had just opened for duck and partridge. Had I heard of the developments in South Connemara, where duck were being stocked, released and fed for monthly shoots? I had not, typically. Nor had I heard of novel plans to get farmers in the area to grow a variety of root crops and mustard in which to foster partridge. These schemes made our own local game clubs pheasant stocking programme appear rather conservative. However, we might be able to learn from others' experiments Malachy's interest in gamebirds was confined to obtaining feathers with which to tie his own fishing flies.

Talk turned to more general topics. Phelim ventured that, "Batman had got a queer drenching trying to prevent that poor seal from doing what Nature directed." This had become the talk of the town, providing many a chuckle at Batman's expense. In his role as Park Ranger he had received a call to rescue a beached seal on Renvyle strand, where quite a crowd had gathered to await the arrival of skilled help. Batman and his colleague Gerry Park had summed up the situation at a glance. The seal had not simply been washed ashore. It had come in to die, as seals do. But to say so would have given awful affront to its assembly of wellwishers ... For hour upon freezing hour Batman and Gerry had stood up to their waists in the perishing Atlantic, retrieving the stricken seal each time it allowed the waves to wash it to its deathbed and refloating it again and again, until, at last, the onlookers had grown bored and dispersed. The seal had duly carried out its deathwish, though not before the two lads had nearly caught their own deaths from pneumonia!

Then there was the alarming matter of Geoffrey's "buzzards". Malachy became voluble, "Them yokes'd ate ye. D'ye know the size o' them things!" It hadn't actually happened, yet. But, yes, Geoffrey had spoken of introducing wild American turkeys to these parts, on the basis that pheasant shooting was too one-sided. These brutes—larger than the traditional bronze turkey—were something else altogether. They had been known to attack their assailants. It would be more akin to bull fighting! But what would they live on? "Sure I suppose there's enough sheep around to keep them in comfort for years and years. As long as they wouldn't go for the children ..." Phelim averred. Malachy became even more agitated. His children were still small. Phelim became mischievous.

"I wouldn't mind,"—his children were grown up—"but it was fine and quiet round here since the eagles were got rid of off Muilrea mountain. They took their quare share o' childer. Off to Clare Island beyond in Clew Bay. On the high cliffs, where none could rescue them. Fed them to the eaglets an' all, so they did. Them was the days!" Only the timely appearance of a fresh pint steadied Malachy's fraying nerves. Lucky, too, that Geoffrey seldom frequented the Anglers' Rest. Phelim had obviously read that wondrous book, *Wild Sports Of The West*, written by the sporting parson W. H. Maxwell and rarely out of print since its publication way back in 1843. Set in North Connemara and Mayo, "Wild Sports" is required reading for a vivid and often incredible picture of game fishing and shooting in these parts in the years leading up to the Famine. *Letters from the Irish Highlands*, by the Blakes of Renvyle is another sine qua non for anyone interested in trying to achieve an understanding of Connemara and its indigenous populace.

That "understanding" is essentially for us "blow-ins" to strive to acquire. Failure to do so would leave us forever at odds with our surroundings. Even I could see that. It shouldn't be impossible, in the way that getting to grips with the Cantonese psyche out in Macau had been. But it couldn't be taken as an inevitable consequence of simply frequenting the same few pubs that serve this peninsula. No way. In my favour, I hoped at any rate, was one tenuous thread of ancient local association, on my maternal grandmother's side. She had been a Duane. Her family had come to Connemara in the Middle Ages, as stewards to the O'Flaherty clan, rulers of North Connemara until the Elizabethan conquest of Ireland and a power among a subject people for centuries subsequently. Gogarty referred to his in-laws in "Sackville Street". With the Gogarty Society "convention" looming ever closer, it was high time to find out more about those in-laws ...

While the Duane home, Garranbaun House, had long since passed into other hands and Rossdhu had been pulled down, I had heard of Duanes who had entered the Convent of Mercy in Clifden. My octogenarian Gogarty uncle had observed that the Duanes had spent a thousand years going broke in Connemara, adding that one at least had sought the sanctuary of the convent in response to being eyed up by a MAN! The convent seemed an obvious place to begin my search.

Founded from Galway in 1854, the Convent of Mercy stands high upon a hill on the eastern edge of Clifden and is utterly unmistakable for what it is—a convent. The door was opened by a deceptively youthful Sister Aloysius. Yes, Sister Aloysius remembered Sister Mary Regius.

"But I have read that my great-great-aunt died in 1935, Sister."

"Indeed, young man. But I was admitted in 1931."

Here was the recipe for longevity. Renounce the world. Join an Order! My informant could have passed for an age with myself.

The convent records revealed that Margaret Duane entered

the Convent of Mercy, Clifden, in 1864, at the age of twenty, receiving the name Sr. Mary Regius a year later and being professed a nun in 1867. At the time of her death in 1935 she had spent over seventy years in that establishment, without, in Sr. Aloysius's considered opinion, ever venturing down the main street of Clifden! Her sister, Mary Duane, had followed in her footsteps one year later, duly receiving the name Sr. Mary Philomena. She had gone to her eternal reward relatively young, dying in 1891. Both women must have been born at the height of the Famine, which hit the Clifden area harder than anywhere else, as local historians attest.

My grandmother, niece of these nuns, had been born in 1876, marrying, after a brief courtship it seems, in 1906, a "medical student", as Oliver St. John Gogarty is described in the Registry of Marriage. Both bride and groom are noted as being of "full" age, while the bride's father's "rank or profession" is stated as simply "Gentleman". Bernard Joseph Duane was in fact an American civil war pensioner. One of his ancestors, James Duane, had been the first Mayor of New York after the American Revolution, while another, Mathew, had been a member of Lincoln's Inn and a Governor of the British Museum, an unusual distinction for an Irish Catholic in the eighteenth century. In more recent times my great uncle, also Mathew, had dominated the "flapping" scene in the west of Ireland with cast-off racehorses. Perhaps that's where the racing bug had come from.

October

✎.

M y reward at the end of a working day on the island involved slipping across the lake and down the switchback four miles to Letterfrack for "cocktails", as the consumption of pints of Guinness is euphemistically called. With the days now drawing in, the guilt of wasting daylight hours disappeared at early dusk. What with the twins being away at boarding schools and Milady still working in Kylemore with the last stragglers of the dying tourist season, my only social contact most days occurred during these evening expeditions. True, there was the telephone. Hardly the same thing.

Avuncular, silver-haired Lewis is an early-evening regular, his "cocktail hour" determined by the necessity to return the family motor car to his wife, so that she can arrive to take charge of the bar at seven o'clock each evening. In an earlier life they managed pubs in the London area. Lewis is a local from nearby Ballynakill, while his wife is from Sligo, and thus a "blow-in", for all that she has married into this locality and reared her family here. Retired now, Lewis is a willing raconteur of local folklore, with personal recollections of three generations of the Duanes of Garranbaun, his erstwhile neighbours on the next peninsula south of here. Lewis's reaction to yet another published version of "Garraunbaun" would be worth hearing.

According to Diarmaid Ó Muirithe in his weekly column in *The Irish Times*, "garraun" means a gelding, and is from the Irish "gearrán", from "gearradh", to cut. Carleton has it in *The Party Fight and Funeral* in the compound "garrane-bane", which he glosses for us. His sentence is: "Would you have me for to show the garrane-bane and lave them like a cowardly thraitor?" He explained: "Garrane-bane, the white horse i.e. wanting in mettle. Tradition affirms that James the Second escaped on a white horse from the Battle of the Boyne, and from this circumstance a white horse has become a symbol of cowardice."

"Bless my soul, but you can't believe what you might read in a Protestant paper! Our Garranbaun is a Lake Horse, a creature that lives in Garranbaun Lake. As much of it as you can see above the water looks exactly like a horse. At least the one that I saw in Cartron Lake did. There's this cave at our end of the lake that goes on forever, they say. 'Twas in there he went."

"You've actually seen a Lake Horse?" And what else besides, I wondered, intrigued. "A long time ago it was. Like the giant eel. You know all about that lad, of course? Fifteen foot long he is. And when he wants to travel from Cartron to Garranbaun he swims ashore, puts his tail into his mouth, turns himself into a wheel and cycles himself across by my house the half mile from one lake to the other. You can follow his track by the slime he leaves after him." Pacing his narrative, with one eye on that domineering clock above the bar, Lewis depleted his pint to that critical point between half-full and half-empty and gestured for its successor.

Batman introduced himself with a query to Lewis on the subject of the beheaded, re-headed saint from Lewis's locality. "That is quite true. St. Ceannanach was beheaded on a rock behind us in Ballynew. The bloodstain is on the rock yet. He picked up his severed head, walked over to the well in the field, washed it and put it back on his shoulders, where it rightly belonged. As he went on his way he declared that happiness would never visit that area ... Prior of Ross House was a godless man. Believed in nothing nor no one. He ordered his men to fill in the well, and in those days they had to obey. The very next morning Prior was out into the yard, roused his men and told them to re-open the well and build a protective wall around it. What had that heathen seen in the night?"

On that dramatic note Lewis drained his pint and withdrew from our midst, for the witching hour was nigh. We talked instead of the Arctic skuas seen circling over Tully Lake in recent weeks and the strange phenomenon of egrets spotted along these shores and the "Chinese" goose that had taken up residence on Renvyle Lake. But I was curious about this man Prior, the "heathen" from Ross House.

Beyond The Twelve Bens, by Kathleen Villiers-Tuthill, a native of Clifden, revealed that one Thomas Young Prior had owned 1,084 acres on the shores of Ballinakill Bay in 1871. Following Prior's death in 1894 his widow, Honoria, had sold 1,140 statute acres to the Armstrong-Lushington-Tullochs of nearby Shanbolard Hall. The new owners noted: "The entire estate abounds with game, pheasants, partridge, hares, rabbits, wild duck and in winter cock, snipe, widgeon and teal. Fishing: herring, cod, haddock and whiting during winter and gunner, mackerel, bream and pollock from May to September, with first rate lobster fishing on the shores and rocks adjoining the land." Proof indeed of the "heathen" Prior's existence. Encouragement, too, that partridge could be viable in Connemara once again.

Lewis was not alone in the curfew stakes, for Milady was averse to pouring glasses of petrol into the generator as the only means of getting the wretched thing to ignite. Thus the production of dinner each evening required my presence sometime in advance of the appointed hour, in my role of mechanic-cum-sorcerer by flashlight in the recesses of the toolshed. Each attempt invoked more curses on the tousled head of the elusive Paud.

Milady was becoming nightly less enamoured of her situation, attributing its shortcomings succinctly to her spouse … If "proper" electrification was beyond my powers, could I perhaps devote even a tiny portion of my unquestionable intellect to the pressing problem of WINDOWS? To be more precise, could I rectify—forthwith—a situation whereby attempts to heat this "rookery of a house" constituted an infinitely greater task; raising the air temperature of the whole of bloody Connemara! Milady had a point. Going to bed each night was as if running the gauntlet: taking a bath invited double pneumonia.

The quest for estimates provoked the by-now-accustomed series of reactions. "Heather Island, you said. Is that on AN ISLAND, like? It must be in the sea, so. And this is October, you know."

"Yes, our house is on an island, but it's a lake island. No problem getting across, generally."

You can tell from a man's expression when belief has become suspended and that impression of sheer incredulity is confirmed when the men in question are invited to clamber into a small rowing boat to cross to an invisible abode obscured in trees. Only one of those canvassed seemed at all confident of his company's ability to carry out the commission. The others threw bids on it in the same way that I had approached the generator with the initial quarter-cup of petrol—fearfully.

Double-glazed windows are buoyant. Well, they don't actually sink. We established this to our satisfaction and the supplier's visible relief when the first consignment slid off the gunwales of the big Culfin Anglers' boat and into the lake. The difference their installation made was instant and tangible. How had we ever survived without these miracles of modern insulation? The heat level soared. The noise level—in windy conditions—sank to inaudibility. Nothing rattled in its old, familiar fashion. Doors no longer slammed shut as others were wrenched open. It was all distinctly disconcerting. While luxuriating in this unaccustomed comfort, I began to fear that the old house might feel affronted.

Not, of course, that this affront would manifest itself in any malevolent way. It simply wasn't that sort of house. Besides, pyschic disturbances had never been on our agenda. Never. Anyway, the master bedroom had not been re-equipped, being only recently refurbished. There the nearly-new steel windows (1920s) still rattled and moaned, weeping puddles of condensation and rainwater, while the curtains billowed in the draughts induced by increasingly frequent southeasterlies.

Paud was delighted for us. "You won't know yourselves with those new windows. They're the greatest thing since the sliced pan. The heat'll be runnin' off yous! My missus'll give me some stick when she hears what you're after doing in there."

"Paud, there'll be more than your missus after your blood, if you don't get the island switched on!" The same abashed smile, swiftly replaced by a hunted look, as Paud thought of all the other increasingly irate madams to whom he had blithely promised miracles, "agin the Christmas" ...

"Sure, haven't you the Gogarty thing coming up shortly? Time enough for me to be goin' in there, tearing the place apart again. Leave it till after that, anyhow." Tossing off his pint, Paud had beaten a strategic retreat, more than ever like the Flying Dutchman, condemned to sail the seas forever, unwelcome in any port. This "tearing the place apart" sounded ominous. What had been airily described as "finishing touches" was coming to suggest major surgery.

Paud's counter-punch had landed all the same, and well he knew it. The Gogarty Society "convention" in Renvyle House loomed ever closer and much remained to be done. Rupert's rounding up of the usual suspects had run into problems, not least because these literary lions had demonstrated a distinct aversion to sharing the limelight with one another. Acceptance by one seemed to trigger off waspish refusals from another. Deliverance came from an unexpected quarter. Count John McCormack came to the rescue. It was his grandfather's anniversary. The great tenor had been among the first guests to stay when Renvyle had opened its doors as an hotel in 1930. Finbar Wright, Ireland's leading contemporary tenor, would sing a programme of McCormack's melodies, given a suitable venue ...

Milady mooted this possibility to the Community in Kylemore. What a wonderful way to commission the recently restored and re-dedicated Gothic Chapel, built in the grounds of Kylemore as a memorial to his late wife by a disconsolate Mitchell Henry in 1875. The ritual process of consultation duly completed, the Community gave its consent. Now we had a double-header. Many years before, while both students at Trinity, Johnny McCormack and I had discussed the possibility of forming Famous Grandfathers Inc., with which to tour America in the footsteps of our illustrious forebears and by this means curing the chronic complaints of penury that dogged us then. Later on came the realisation that penury is indeed a permanent condition, from which temporary remissions are occasionally obtained, but permanent release never.

Renvyle House had seen nothing like it since its high society opening in 1930, when the rich and famous had assembled to toast the Gogartys' success in their new venture. To a packed and sparkling audience Professor Derry Jeffares unveiled John Coll's recently-completed bust of Oliver St John Gogarty, portrayed in characteristically discursive pose. The Galway-born sculptor and his wife had flown over from

Amsterdam for the occasion, while from America had come Maggie Williams (coincidentally), daughter of Dr. William Spickers, who had befriended Gogarty during his prolonged exile in the States. With her was Hurd Hatfield, famous for his starring role in *The Picture of Dorian Gray*. Later that opening night Ulick O'Connor excelled himself in his performance of *The last of the Bucks*, his one-man show relating the life and work of Gogarty, whose first biographer Ulick had been, some thirty years before. In the time-honoured Renvyle tradition of "hould your hour and have another", well-lubricated conviviality was punctuated by sporadic outpourings of Kraken's golden trumpet.

Any fears of anti-climax the following day were soon dispelled by Michael Gibbons's Pied Piper-like safari around the Renvyle peninsula, his running commentary ranging, at lightning speed, from the Bronze Age to de Valera, with a thread of tenuous continuity that moved one wag, Aidan Heavey, to recall Gogarty's assertion: "Of course Dev's Irish. Doesn't he resemble a capital letter uncurled from the Book of Kells!"

Those who knew my grandfather well always claimed that the deaths of his close friends, Arthur Griffith and Michael Collins, had permanently blighted his sunny nature, causing him to become increasingly embittered as he grew older. Gogarty laid the blame for the deaths of both Griffith and Collins firmly at de Valera's door. As a Senator in the first Irish Free State Government Gogarty had never missed an opportunity to vilify de Valera, that "sixpenny Savonarola". His own kidnapping, his enforced exile in London and the burning of Renvyle in 1923 he similarly attributed to his arch-enemy. In *As I Was Going Down Sackville Street* he wrote: "I blame it on the Long Fellow listening to that little yellow bittern. Look at us now! We have lost in fourteen years what it took forty to achieve: fixity of tenure for farmers and our fiscal freedom. Freedom is hard to come by, but harder still to hold. If de Valera was in the pay of England's secret service he couldn't do Ireland half the harm that he is doing it now."

Gogarty's attacks on de Valera in the Senate have passed into legend for their very vituperation. To that "Laugh in mourning ... that cross between a cormorant and a corpse", Gogarty had addressed this warning: "Therefore, I tell you to have a care, President de Valera, lest your silhouette may come to be regarded as the most sinister which ever darkened the light in genial Ireland and that it may not be without ominous significance that, during the election, your name was written on the dead walls and roofless ruins of this, our Country."

De Valera had had the last laugh, if, indeed, he ever indulged in such audible expressions of pleasure. He dissolved the Senate, leaving Gogarty to reflect bitterly in *Sackville Street*: "Renvyle House is burned by the I.R.A. The long, long house in the ultimate land of the undiscovered West. Why should they burn my house? Because I am not an Irishman? because I do not flatter fools? If the only Irishman who is allowed to live in Ireland must be a bog-trotter, then I am not an Irishman. And I object to the bog-trotter being the ideal exemplar of all Irishmen. I refuse to conform to that type."

So saying, Gogarty had taken himself into self-imposed exile in the United States, writing to his friend, Shane Leslie: "Saddened by the drabness, misery and meanness of my natal city under the exclusive Commune, I, finding myself the only householder in a cul-de-sac of tenements, sold Ely Place to that treble contradiction in terms the Royal Hibernian Academy. The Institution is to turn my garden into a non-Platonic Academe and build its picture gallery thereon."

Gogarty's years in exile were recalled by Maggie Williams in her moving address at his graveside in Ballynakill, overlooking Cartron Lake, where she described his kindliness and charm to her in her teenage years as well as his underlying loneliness for his native Ireland. Maggie subsequently presented us with a copy of Gogarty's portrait by Gerald Brockhurst, never previously seen on this side of the Atlantic. The Brockhurst portraits of Gogarty's wife and children had always been in the family, but this was an absolute bolt from the blue; a circle at last complete.

It was time to switch the emphasis from one illustrious forebear to another. During our odyssey around Gogarty's beloved Connemara, Milady and her willing helpers had decked out the Gothic Chapel in Kylemore in preparation for its finest hour. All was in readiness; the baby grand piano, the pianist, Angel Chiment, and, crucially, Ireland's leading tenor, Finbar Wright. The atmosphere in the miniature cathedral became more charged by the moment as Mother Abbess and her Community took their seats alongside Count John McCormack and his Countess, Sylvia, with members and guests filling the tiny auditorium to be welcomed by Milady, radiant in her cherished role as apostle of this architectural masterpiece, dearer to her even than her own home.

By inclination more aligned to Publicans than Pharisees, I had chosen to sit at the back of the church. It proved an inspired decision, for the perfect acoustics of this amazing edifice ensured that Finbar's mellifluous, majestic tenor voice came rolling in great waves of sound from the chancel where he sang along the vaulted roof to wash down upon those of us at the furthest end of the nave. Often have I read of "out of body experiences" ... Now I realised the meaning of that arcane expression. A beaming Mother Abbess disclosed, during the interval, that this very day was the thirtieth anniversary of her admission to the Kylemore Community.

Over dinner in Renvyle House that night both Finbar and Angel were emphatic that within moments of their starting to perform each had become infected by the extraordinary atmosphere of the Gothic Chapel and the almost tangible enthusiasm of their audience. Finbar, said Angel, had achieved heights that he had never approached in the most sophisticated of recording studios, while Angel, Finbar averred, had seldom, if ever, accomplished such a mixture of tacit strength and subtlety in his accompaniment. Octogenarian Maureen Roche, an utterly unlikely innkeeper from Donaghadea, paid Finbar the ultimate compliment ... She had been present at John McCormack's final concert in the Albert Hall in 1938. Finbar, she declared, had done the maestro justice!

Watching Finbar, still on a "high" after his virtuoso performance, beaming his appreciation of a succession of heartfelt compliments from people as inflamed by the occasion as he was himself, it was impossible to imagine what emotions raged beneath that smiling exterior. Here was a former priest, now married with a young family, celebrating one of his finest singing performances, staged in a church, before an audience of nuns. The very table at which he was seated only compounded this irony. Behind his head hung a huge picture by Galway artist Mary Waters. It portrayed in graphic detail the wedding feast of Dionysus and Ariadne, eschewing all vestiges of feminine modesty. It was a scenario that the once and former owner of Renvyle House would hardly have allowed to pass without comment.

As with all festive gatherings, the "morning after" session produced its batch of mishaps ... Rupert had been verbally abused by one of his literary lions, who claimed that he had been unforgivably "overshadowed", to such a degree that redress might well be sought through recourse to the Law. Poor Maureen had found herself unaccountably locked into her bedroom on the second floor and was only forestalled at the last moment from shinning to freedom down a potentially lethal rope of bedclothes that she had knotted together. The doctor from Athenry sheepishly revealed that his "pulled muscle", sustained in following Michael Gibbons over ditches and dykes to the site of the standing stones high above Tully Lake, was in fact a broken leg.

Inevitably there were disgruntled wives, whose husbands had neglected their matrimonial responsibilities in their determination to prove they were not "Irish queers"—defined as men who prefer women to drink. The shrewdly experienced manager of Renvyle House, had counselled Bucks' Fizz as the "sovreign remedie" for such occasions. And so it proved. Threatened divorce proceedings dissolved in light-hearted misgivings as to our ability to lay on a comparable event a year hence. But we worried not. A lot could happen in the intervening twelve months, as Time, in turn, would show.

The ending of the Gogarty "Octoberfest", as we had styled that event, also marked the end of Summer Time, plunging us into long evenings of unwelcome darkness, for which we were ill-equipped, still dependent for illumination on the vagaries of that infernal combustion engine, when it consented to combust. Paud Ruane was more than ever a marked man, with a price on his head. That price was not difficult to compute, for the generator guzzled petrol to the tune of one pound (punt) per hour. To drive to Galway, pay admission to a cinema and drive the fifty-six miles back to Renvyle would, we calculated, cost no more than to watch a similar amount of television in the "comfort" of Heather Island. As a compromise we joined the Letterfrack Film Club, for their winter season of "cult" and "genre" films. These proved to be entertaining in their sheer awfulness, reminiscent of those bizarre outpourings of Hongkong TV experienced in Macau.

Compounding our growing sense of isolation was Milady's receipt of the dreaded DCM (Don't come in on Monday). Kylemore Abbey, outlet for her prodigious energies and source of revenue for the summer season, was closing down at Hallowe'en. Left thus at a loose end, high but seldom dry, Milady would find time lying heavily on her hands, increasingly imprisoned by that forbidding cordon of turbulent water, in a house from which the term "home" was as yet withheld, her friends a hundred miles distant or more. That the shooting season was about to open impressed her not at all. Milady doesn't shoot — at pheasants anyway. A distraction was urgently required.

It duly manifested itself in the form of a telephone call from the founder of "Hidden Ireland", that monocled master of make-believe, John Colclough. Months ago, it seemed now in the dying days of October, we had sought his advice on the viability of enrolling in his organisation of out-of-the-way country houses, providing sustenance and accommodation to intrepid travellers all over Ireland. At the time John had not been overly enthusiastic in his response, wondering aloud at the attractions of an island in Connemara, other than in the height of summer. However, he had said that he would run his (monocled) eye over our place whenever his travels should take him this far west of his comfortable Dublin abode. That time was nigh and he would have one of the top executives from the Irish Tourist Board in tow. I panicked. "Great. But are you quite sure? The weather's getting very dicey and we haven't got the ESB switched on yet. Maybe you should wait until the spring. The island's looking very bare and inhospitable."

This elegant advocate of the power of positive thinking was not to be dissuaded. They were on their way and would be here in time for lunch. Milady was incensed. "Is the man mad, like you? Hasn't he heard the forecast, effing force eight! And I've no food in the house." In truth, that forecast was redundant. The promised gale had arrived. Through the leafless, tossing branches I could all too easily see the waves sweeping down the lake, driven by heightening southwesterly winds, punctuated by those dreaded gusts that render the best of boats uncontrollable in the fury of their passing.

Bernice reiterated Milady's reservations upon my sanity as I ransacked the shelves of the shop in search of victuals to serve our visitors, puddles forming around my feet at the counter. Bernice knew my great-uncle, Mattie Duane, to have been eccentric, but he had at least lived on dry land. At the appointed hour our visitors arrived down to the boathouse, where I sheltered from horizontal sheets of rain, the gusts now separated by seconds rather than minutes. This crossing would not be easy. It would take time, and effort. The big Culfin Anglers' boat seemed a safer bet. Monocled John wore tweeds, his companion a light city suit ... Only partly protected by ill-fitted macks of ours and half strangled by our recently acquired lifejackets, they took their thwarts with visible trepidation. The man from the Tourist Board had turned a very unhealthy colour.

The worst stretch of this crossing is in the middle, out of the shelter of the shore and not yet in the lee of the island. This bit always seems to take forever in foul weather. The secret is not to panic; just keep rowing into the wind, gaining a few yards between each squall. The man from the Tourist Board became visibly perturbed, more so when John Colclough—the rain streaming down his monocle—began singing at the top of his voice, "Nearer my God to thee, nearer to thee ..."

Never have I witnessed jorums of Jameson so gratefully seized and so swiftly depleted as sodden clothing steamed furiously in front of the fire. The man from the Tourist Board was emphatic. He would not be sending any of his inspectorate to Heather Island. John Colclough had proved his reliability in assessing his Hidden Houses. If he said Heather Island met the standards required, then so be it. Having regained the safety of the shore in a lull between gusts, the man from the Tourist Board wished me luck with Heather Island, counselling against sinking too much money into such a venture. I took his point.

The onset of Hallowe'en signalled the physical closing-down of Connemara, into what was to be a six-month hibernation. The ubiquitous B & B signs disappeared from their mountings along the roadsides. The summer restaurants had already closed, shuttered now until Easter. Clifden seemed to have more shop windows barren than dressed. Those that remained trading now invited their reduced clientele to join their Christmas Clubs, to lessen the financial pain on the run-up to that great winter orgy of spending. Renvyle House, under a skeleton staff, became quite eerie to enter; dust sheets draped where scantily clad tourists had roamed weeks previously.

And Milady was thrown once more on her husband's increasingly slender resources, no more to traverse Greenmount daily, passing the hamlet of Currywongaun, tucked away in a fold of the foothills of Duchruach. One of the gems of local folklore Milady had garnered from her workmates in Kylemore concerned the solitary, un-named, two-storeyed house in Currywongaun. The legend has it that the elderly occupants of this house were beguiled into making it over to relations from faraway Westport, on the understanding that they would be cared for till the end of their days in return. The usurpers promptly threw their benefactors into the workhouse in Clifden. Incensed by this act of treachery and betrayal, the local priest prevailed upon the newcomers to honour their undertaking in spirit as well as letter. Rebuffed, the cleric declared: "No cradle will ever rock in this house." Since that angry exchange, over one hundred years ago, no child has ever been born into that house.

A glimpse such as that behind the curtain that separates blow-ins from the indigenous populace is worth more than all the published pieces on these parts. That she should have been told it at all was a tribute to Milady's relatively swift acceptance by the "regulars" of Kylemore Abbey's tourist season team, mostly locals working there for years. In truth

Milady was already able to put many more names to faces throughout the locality than could I, for all that I had summered down here since childhood. One of those "bright young things", so prevalent in the pages of newspapers nowadays, wrote recently on the respective roles of cohabiting men and women: "There's a good reason why women dress like lumberjacks these days. It's because we ARE fucking lumberjacks, we even do our own decorating. We're coping, while they're making big plans." Guilty as charged, your honour. "And no, your honour, Heather Island isn't quite ready to be called 'home' to my wife and family. But we're nearly there ... What with the ESB getting switched on, the new boat I've ordered and our furniture from England, they won't know themselves. By Christmas the job'll be Oxo, your honour!"

This Christmas deadline was catching. Had I not just used it myself? But first there was Hallowe'en, half-term for the twins. Milady travelled to Galway to meet them from their respective bus and train. We would rendezvous in the Renvyle Inn, for the weather forecast was ominous; "Southwesterly gales along the West coast from Slyne Head to Malin Head, gusting at times to eighty miles per hour." Each time the door of the pub blew open to admit another dishevelled wayfarer, his advent brought forth a chorus of muttered forebodings; "It's gettin' into a whoor of a night." One part of me wanted my family to materialise forthwith. The other yearned for a 'phone call announcing their intention to spend the night in Galway. Excellent as ever, the pint of Guinness in that storm-lashed hostelry held little pleasure that evening. My chickens were coming home to roost—in more ways than one.

The big old Anglers' boat tossed in the darkness at the pier, as wave after wave crashed invisibly on the rocks around us. We would use two sets of oars; luggage in the bows, twins in the stern. I would take her out into the blackness on one set and get the bows turned to face our invisible destination.

Milady would then pick up on my stroke, despite operating astern of me. That isn't easy, less so when you've never rowed tandem, in the teeth of a gale. The middle of the crossing was the worst. Waves began breaking over the bow gunwale, drenching our backs as we heaved and strained to make headway, more and more water sloshing around our feet. A momentary gap in the clouds provided a silhouette of the twins, huddled together in mutual succour against the rain and the spray. Ages later we landed, exhausted. No word was spoken as we unloaded the old boat by wavering torchlight, already fretful in the confines of our lifejackets, nor as we squelched up through pools of water to the shelter of the house and a wondering welcome from the waiting animals, impatient to be fed.

For all that they had been away at school throughout the descent from autumn to winter, the twins needed no bidding to bank the stoves, light more fires, get the gas heaters going and the curtains drawn, before attending to their own comforts. Mercifully, the generator roared into life with its infusion of petrol into the cylinder, providing light for Milady to put dinner in the oven. The twins' bedrooms reverberated to blasts of "heavy metal", "grunge" or whatever. Frayed nerves soothed by badly needed drinks, we could congratulate ourselves on overcoming the elements, however foolhardy I might have been. Milady said little, busying herself around her kitchen, for there was little that needed to be said. Married for more years than we had been single, each of us had long since come to appreciate the potency of silence in situations where speech can trigger explosion, and cannot be retracted.

Some time during the night the slates on the western end of the house were blown off. Their splintered remains embedded in tree trunks told the tale. Had I encountered one when venturing outside to knock off the generator it could have beheaded me, for these were the old-fashioned, genuine, quarried slates, no longer used, for obvious reasons. They are lethal in such circumstances. Like the scales of a salmon, they had peeled from above the gutter to halfway up a particularly inaccessible portion of the roof. Below it was the old kitchen, single-storeyed and roofed with asbestos sheeting, impossible to walk upon. From the high bank to the west of the house I could see that it would take but little to strip the rest of that section of the roof. Untended for years, the slates had been sheltered from the worst of the winds by an enormous fallen macrocarpa. But I, in my wisdom, had cut up the macrocarpa, declaring it unsightly and fit only for firewood.

Malachy Kane rose magnificently to the challenge. "We may take out the window on the return o' the stairs and run the scaffold out through it. 'Tis the only way at it. If we wedge her 'athin and brace her beyont agin' the bank, it could take yous out o' yer troubles, so it could, now!" It seemed there was nothing else for it. While I went to Clifden to fetch slates, Malachy tore out the window in question. The temperature indoors plummeted, our smart new windows mocked by the icy blasts that funnelled up and down the stairwell. As Malachy shouted his demands from his eyrie above the window space, the twins and I scurried to and fro, bearing squares of felt, slating laths, nails and finally the slates themselves. From the ground Malachy resembled a lizard, as he writhed and squirmed to marry the new slates with the old and stabilise the whole expanse. The window didn't go back quite as it had been before. They never do, quite.

The twins had adapted well to their boarding school regime, but for a credibility problem among their peers. It had to do with their living on an island. "Nobody lives on islands, nowadays. They don't have to anymore. You're making it up. Liar, liar, liar!" And the more that each would insist that this was the case, the more he or she was ridiculed. As if having lived in Macau wasn't enough! Mindful of her own schoolgirl problems of non-acceptance through having a racehorse trainer for a father, Milady readily identified with her twins' predicament. The difference between her situation and theirs was simple. Her father, I was invited to agree, had trained racehorses for his livelihood, whereas I had chosen to live on this island, without any idea of earning my livelihood. "Do I make myself perfectly plain?" "Perfectly clear, my dear. For 'plain' you could never be described!" Co-existence without the buffer of children after all those years demanded a delicacy, a deftness, a degree of diplomacy reflecting Harold Pinter's memorable line: "Marriage is a habit, not a passion."

November

⁂

Nicholas and Camellia returned to school willingly enough, having extracted from me a promise that I had not the first notion how to honour. I would get our household belongings across from Leeds in time for Christmas. Wouldn't I? It was a very tempting idea, if impractical with the onset of winter. Even if two twenty-foot containers could be got down to the boathouse — and that was a very big "If" — there was no space to offload them and no means of removing them once emptied. All of us coveted something different; the twins their artefacts with which to make their bedrooms as they had had them in Yorkshire, Milady her treasured furnishings and I my library. But how? Milady was adamant. It could be done. She would resolve the problem. Just get the stuff across. I should have smelled a rat ...

Stalling, as usual, I suggested we slip over to Yorkshire and collect our pictures, stored separately in a friend's house in Ripon. Their repatriation and distribution about the house brought the realisation of "home" one step closer. But it did not suffice. The combination of austere oak furniture — "Pugin", one of our Gogarty Society visitors had described it — and exhausted armchairs and sofas (not to mention beds), unremarked over twenty summer vacations, did not constitute "home". What was I waiting for? Mollified by my reluctant compliance, Milady set about readying the house for Christmas.

An unexpected covering of sleet on the slopes of Muilrea heralded the onset of winter proper and the need for something a bit livelier than turf to keep the home fires burning. The island was covered in fallen timber and our near neighbour, stout, bearded Mike Killeen had a chainsaw. A blow-in like ourselves (he was from Athlone), Mike had built himself a bolt-hole surrounded by fir trees at the western end of the lake, a place to rest up between engineering assignments the world over. A serious-minded man, Mike did not lightly embark upon the business of cutting timber. Steel-capped leather boots, gauntlets, safety helmet and visor had all to be donned ere cutting could commence. His current cautionary tale concerned the farmer who had turned to shout instructions to 'er indoors, swinging his chainsaw as he did so, unaware that his young son was standing behind him …

Now I realised why I had never invested in one of these fearsome contraptions. It wasn't only my fear of denuding the island of timber. As fast as I fed the fallen logs on to the "horse", Mike sawed them into lengths for splitting and feeding to our voracious stoves. I was to discover that fuel consumption increases in direct relation to the quantity to hand under the veranda. Thus enlightened, I began to hoard supplies where they had been assembled, bringing barrow-loads up to the house as and when required. A fire performs as well half-full as brim-full, while only consuming half the quantity of timber.

Mike seemed happy to keep cutting my timber. As he said himself, he and his family were moving to San Diego after Christmas, to a new project, where opportunities to wield his chainsaw were unlikely to abound. He loved Connemara, but couldn't see a way to making a living down here. No more than myself, he could never grow tired of the scenery. But he couldn't live off it. He was likewise intrigued by the social history of the area, increasingly highlighted in the media as a consequence of the 150th anniversary of the Famine. Had I seen Alan Harman's piece on Mary Sammon's memorial stone, "To the memory of the little children", erected recently on a bluff called Sméaróg, on the shoreline near Renvyle Hotel? Seen it? I'd been down to the site to convince myself that what I had read was true.

On Tim Robinson's invaluable map, "Connemara", there are sites marked simply "CBG". The initials stand for "Children's Burial Ground", unconsecrated graveyards, indicated by crude mounds of sea stones. Some sixty years earlier, Mary Sammon, a frail but indomitable octogenarian, had been delivered of stillborn twins. Unbaptised, they could not be interred in a Catholic graveyard. Stephen, her late husband, had carried the two tiny coffins down to this plot that had originated in Famine times and buried them in a sod fence. In Mary Sammon's words: "I organised the memorial because I knew they should have gone into the consecrated ground and not be thrown into sod fences. There are babies from all over the area in the grave. But none have been buried there in recent years. I don't think people nowadays would allow it."

Shaking his head in disbelief, Mike had drained his mug of coffee, put his pipe back in his pocket and tugged the chainsaw back to life. Born into the Church of Rome, Mike Killeen had seen enough of the world, and of the Church in Holy Ireland to appreciate the chasm between Catholicism and Christianity.

During our next respite he reminded me of the definition of an Irish Catholic—one who prays on his knees on Sundays and preys on his neighbours the other six days of the week. As for "Hemingway" Harman, the writer of the article and Mary Sammon's tenant … What can he have thought; this visitor to our shores? Maybe his outpourings in pubs about Ireland being a Third World country, disbarred only by its climate, weren't that wide of the mark.

"Hemingway" was in my thoughts for another reason

throughout the first half of November, as the launch date for our *History of the Irish Grand National,* kindly underwritten by the race sponsors, Jameson, drew ever nearer. "Hemingway"—a non-racing man—had commented on the alarming casualty rate among steeplechasers, citing the unfortunate demise of several more recent winners of the race. Noncommittal, I had observed that those things happen in 'chasing, while wondering quite why so many of late seemed to have met their end prematurely. Days before the launch one of the "dead" not only came back to life, but ran and was placed, two years after his reported demise. My co-author was disconcerted, but unrepentant. He had only reiterated what the papers of the day had reported. It was too late to correct our text. An erratum was the only possibility in the time remaining. Borrowing Mark Twain's wry remark, we attributed to "Vanton" these words: "The report of my death was an exaggeration."

Sportingly, trainer Michael O'Brien agreed to bring Vanton, his equine Lazarus, to Fairyhouse racecourse for the launch, where the burly chestnut seemed to relish his TV celebrity status, without the trauma of galloping and jumping for three and a half miles, as he had had to do when winning the Irish National over three years before.

Fairyhouse racecourse in the dying days of November felt quite peculiar. It was one of those "industry days", as they are now described, meaning that only the protagonists turn up and the racegoing public stays away. It was a very far cry from that sunny Easter Monday in 1980 when we had driven "Daletta" up from Tullamore to carry off the Irish Grand National at our first attempt, before a crowd of twenty thousand or more. Now, strolling aimlessly around the deserted enclosures, I sought to recreate the scene. But John Harty, brother-in-law and winning jockey that day, was dead. The lucky owners had dropped out of racing long since and I had not been directly associated with a winner since landing a Bedale point-to-point in North Yorkshire a decade ago. That ghost was well and truly laid. It was timely to return to Connemara, leaving all thoughts of horses and racing firmly east of the Shannon.

Among the year-round resident blow-ins who frequent our adopted "local" in Letterfrack there exists a coded camaraderie. Absences are noted and admonished, unless, of course, caused by a bereavement. After all, death is a way of life in Ireland, and hearse-chasing a social requirement. This explains the abiding popularity of the *Irish Independent* in rural Ireland. It carries all the death notices; *The Irish Times* relatively few. Weaned on the latter paper, we are continually disconcerted to learn of a death in the area some time after interment has taken place. So with our "local". Readmission to the set can be gained only by fulsome explanation for one's disappearance. Anything short of a trip to the moon is perceived as base treachery, and promptly dismissed. The short, reproving silence is then shattered by everybody gabbling at once, each eager to be the first to impart the riveting developments that have taken place during one's defection.

November's "hot gossip" concerned the "Mannin Bay business" ... Caution was called for, in mixed company. Some of the circle would be in favour and others opposed; whatever the proposal. The Clifden-based salmon-farming company had applied for a licence to erect cages off Mannin Bay, one of the most renowned beauty spots along the Connemara coast. This site would be supplementary to four others already in operation, albeit in relatively concealed locations. The community of that area south of Clifden was vociferous in its opposition, as were the shellfish farmers in the vicinity. There was going to be trouble if the licence were granted and the development went ahead. Further discussion was abruptly curtailed by the entrance of one of the partners in the salmon farm, glowering Gerry Fish, a rugby alickadoo. Talk turned diplomatically to the prospects for the season of Connemara's "All Blacks" junior rugby team and their chances of extending their astonishing run of success on their home pitch outside the town, where they had played over seventy consecutive matches without tasting defeat.

Gerry Fish is so called to distinguish him from Gerry Sheep and Gerry Park, also habitués of our Letterfrack "local". Gerry Sheep is a wool merchant and a refugee from County Mayo. He lives in Lettergesh and "ower the blanket", as the Yorkshire expression has it. Gerry Park, a Clareman, is a park ranger, with particular responsibility for the Connemara pony herd in the National Park that covers thousands of acres and encompasses several of the Twelve Bens, the oldest mountains in the world. He is also Batman's boss. Like British policemen, park rangers sport beards.

Gerry Fish seldom talks about his livelihood, and never in general company, for fish farming as a social topic is on a par with drug trafficking or gun running; or so its practitioners seem to feel. Should "shop" need to be discussed, those directly involved fade from the scene at the bar, returning to replenish their glasses, the business of the moment concluded. Gerry Sheep, on the other hand, is much more forthcoming, regaling all and sundry with his epic whiskey-drinking feats of endurance in hillside farmhouses that seldom receive visitors. His stories convey vividly the sense of isolation in which so many elderly bachelors exist on the remote Connemara hillsides, with only their sheepdogs for company. They represent the rump of a deserted generation of men, deprived of any chance of marriage by the mass exodus of their womenfolk to England throughout the 'fifties, 'sixties and even in more recent times. Ironically, many of these girls subsequently returned as married women to their birthplace, bringing "blow-in" husbands in their wake.

One of Gerry Sheep's better yarns (!) concerns a mighty hulk of a man, who owns more land than anyone would care to walk. From sheep subsidies alone this genial giant's income exceeds that of the Taoiseach. In days gone by this lonesome bachelor offered ten thousand pounds, in cash, for any woman's hand in marriage. Finding no takers for what was a comparative fortune, he sought solace in carefully prepared drinking bouts. Before embarking on a week's total inebriation he would purchase seven new shirts, one for each day's drinking around the pubs of Clifden, and cut off the sleeves, for reasons known only to himself. Accommodation would be reserved in the town and arrangements made for a barber to shave him each morning. Rested and refreshed, he would put away a bottle of whiskey before breaking for a midday feed. The afternoon, evening and night would see another bottle consumed, now interspersed with pints. His final port of call on his way back to the hills after such a session is invariably our "local", where tea and sandwiches are made available, but no liquor. However outraged he may become at being refused drink and however loudly he may insult the bar staff, it is absolutely understood by both parties that this particular bash is over, consequently offence is neither given nor taken. Having previously recoiled from the ferocity of these encounters at close hand, we were grateful for Gerry Sheep's clarification of this particular charade.

Not all of Gerry Sheep's suppliers are blessed with the constitutions of oxen, as this man clearly must be. One paid the ultimate penalty for seasonal over-indulgence, falling off his bicycle when in sight of his lonely farmstead and dying of exposure on the side of the boreen. His mourners agreed it was his meanness that killed him, for in his pocket was an uncashed cheque for sheep headage payments to the tune of twenty-four thousand pounds. Anyone less tight-arsed would have bought himself a motorcar and thus survived; so they said. Gerry seeks

off-season respite from sheep farmers, western society and
Smithwicks on the golf courses of Florida and the Canaries,
compounding this social gaffe by reappearing tanned and
invigorated into our pallid mid-winter midst.

Gerry Park is likewise happy to talk about his job, being
careful to use that term rather than employing the word
"work", which could readily give rise to slagging, for
everybody agrees that being a park ranger is the ultimate
sinecure, especially "playing with the ponies". The locals
delight in referring to Gerry as a botanist, as a prelude to
disclosing that in an earlier life Gerry was a postman.
Newcomers to the Connemara scene invariably delude
themselves that nothing is known of their previous existences,
other than that which they choose to disclose. Such notions are
quietly disabused, along with any airs and graces. Not that
Gerry Park—master of the roll-your-own cigarette—suffers
from delusions of grandeur. He doesn't. Rather is he happy to
disseminate the legend of "Cannon Ball", quite literally the
Daddy of them all in the Connemara stud book, the pony from
whom all registered Connemara ponies descend.

Cannon Ball belonged to one "Henri" Toole, of Leam, near
Oughterard. The grey was never defeated in the pony races
that flourished all over Connemara between the wars. Besides
his racecourse feats, Cannon Ball made the weekly journey to
Athenry Market each Saturday, a distance of thirty-two miles
each way, covering any mares presented en route, for a fee of
ten shillings (50p). While Henri sought refreshment in
roadside hostelries, Cannon Ball tucked into his special
mixture—half a dozen eggs in a quart of porter. If drawing a
trap, Cannon Ball simply took his inebriated master home
along the route he knew so well. On the other hand, if Henri
had elected to ride to Athenry, he was prone to topple from the
saddle on the homeward journey. Cannon Ball would catch his
master by his thick frieze coat and shake him out of his stupor,

prior to being remounted and homeward bound once more. Henri on one occasion accepted a wager that Cannon Ball could not beat the Clifden—Galway train over the four-mile stretch from Leam to Oughterard. He collected his bet.

Cannon Ball died, of natural causes, in March 1926, and was "waked" in the traditional fashion, surely the only pony ever to be accorded this honour. Laid out on a stable door, Cannon Ball was borne to his resting place by ten men and interred standing up in a hay-lined grave, overlooking the Oughterard racecourse, scene of so many of his triumphs. His epitaph in *The Connacht Tribune* consisted of these lines:

> "No more with earthly kin you mingle
> Dream of race course tracks you've won,
> Of noble steeds and epic deeds
> And bookies left without a jingle."

Gerry Park's homely, bearded face lights up as he recites those lines, leaving his listeners in no doubt as to his genuine affection for his ponies and their legendary progenitor. While Cannon Ball had no headstone erected to mark his tomb, he has no need of one. His grieving owner planted instead a hawthorn bush, in itself a guarantee that Cannon Ball's grave would never be disturbed, for no right-thinking Irishman would ever cut down or even transplant the fairies' tree. No tree in Ireland is better known or respected for its supernatural associations. Many are the instances in which roads have been diverted to avoid disturbing the lone hawthorn, home and meeting-place of the "little people".

Happily engrossed in conversation on subjects such as these, it is only too tempting to order more pints and defer for a while longer venturing into the darkness of a November evening to face the unseen perils of Tully Lake. After all, perhaps Paud Ruane will drop in and we can extract yet another irrevocable commitment to finish the wiring to the standards demanded by the ESB ... But Milady is adamant. It is time to go. No more fanciful nonsense about gathering material for yet another book never to be written. "The children may be trying to contact us on the telephone. And have we got petrol for the generator? Coyne's will be closed if we don't leave now!" Ah well, 'twas good while it lasted.

People often ask how I can face the lake on a winter's night with drink inside me ... My reply is ever the same. It's a damned sight easier to face it with drink than without. Moreover, the immediate prospect of launching into the darkness and the unknown has a remarkably sobering effect. While it mightn't deceive a breathalyser, it certainly focuses mind and body on the challenge ahead. Would any sane, sensible, practically minded person live this way, for choice? I doubt it. I doubt it very much. And November—I was frequently informed—was but a foretaste of what lay in store when January should come round ...

It was as the month drew to its close that Milady revealed her hand. She had "borrowed" a house on the mainland; "Just as somewhere to put our furniture when it arrives, and maybe we'll be glad of it on really nasty nights." Despite myself I was intrigued. "You've done what? Borrowed a house? Whose house?"

"The Old Schoolhouse in Moyard. Kraken's selling it. It's empty and he agrees it might sell better if it looked lived in." Wow! So that was Milady's solution to the insoluble; how to cope with these two whacking great containers that I had yet to see. If we couldn't accommodate them at our own place, then simply find a more suitable depot, and live in it too! And it had "proper electricity". And you could simply drive right up to the door, as you should be able to do in any "civilised" house.

"Does Kraken's wife know about this wondrous idea?" I had a healthy respect for Kraken's third wife, an outspoken madam from Monaghan, whose forthright views on life in general she managed to contain by her steadfast refusal to accompany her husband to the pub.

"Well, I'm sure Kraken's mentioned it to her. He's bound to have. Isn't he?"

Here was an interesting insight into the female psyche. Milady had inveigled the husband into making his empty house available, leaving him to break the news to his good lady. My mind boggled at the reception I might have met had the situation been the other way around ...

Duly, the two containers arrived at the Old Schoolhouse, in the lee of the Church of Ireland in Moyard, a peaceful and secluded spot, that had served as the tennis club for the Protestant gentry of the area in days gone by. The headstones in the yew-lined graveyard brought Betjeman's lines to mind:

> "There in pinnacled protection,
> One extinguished family waits
> A Church of Ireland resurrection
> By the broken, rusty gates."

True, the gates of St. Thomas's are neither broken nor rusted, but the sense of extinction is very real. Equally real — for the feelings it evokes — is the great, cast iron soup cauldron that squats in the porch of the faded little church, silent reminder of the Famine and the frightful legacy of the laissez faire policy of the government of the day. The names on the plain, unadorned headstones record the passing of the Anglo-Irish Ascendancy in Connemara — Armstrong-Lushington-Tulloch, Browne, Goodbody, Graham, Irwin, Robinson and Thompson. The faded plaques on the walls of the little church tell of husbands and sons who gave their lives for king and country in far-off lands, fighting, purportedly, for the freedom of oppressed peoples, oblivious to the anomaly that their presence in Ireland constituted.

Inevitably the sheer convenience of on-shore domicile during the long nights of darkness swiftly seduced us more and more to overnight in Moyard, surrounded now by all the old familiar trappings of "home" as it had been in other times and places. A routine evolved, whereby we would spend the daylight hours on the island, where so much remained to be done, and the nights in the almost-forgotten luxury of lighting and heating. Fittingly, in view of its title, the Old Schoolhouse had one wall covered by bookshelves, from floor to ceiling. Filling them with my own books was as good as returning to a surprise party of old friends after years abroad. Oh for the day when they should surround me in the south-facing room off the hall on the island, that I had long since marked out as my study.

The dogs, Teal and Plover, for all their lack of years, proved uneasy in our borrowed surroundings and refused to settle. Already accustomed to having the run of their nine-acre, water-girt demesne, with their kennel an upturned packing crate from Macau, they were infinitely more content to be fed and left overnight in the habitat they had clearly made their own. And they had the cat for company. Cats—they say—will not be moved. Not that this one was ever about to be, for the onset of winter invariably brings the water rats around the house, in search of food and even shelter. Having contained their advances thus far, we had no intention of removing our deterrent. Indeed, Milady had begun to talk of getting a second cat, deaf to my murmurings that cats are particularly protective of their own perceived bailiwicks ...

Looking back, November was a lull; idyllic in many ways, our days filled with sifting through our belongings in Moyard and selecting individual pieces to fit in here and there, in what I hoped would prove their permanent home. These we would load into car and trailer, decant into the boat and lug up that path, no longer "crimson-walled by fuchsia", for the fuchsia had long since become denuded. Even the laurel and the rhododendron threatened to become deciduous. Connemara in winter is windswept, on the finest of days. Even on the rare still days, from the lakeshore we could hear the roar of the ocean, invisible and a mile or so distant. It roared to proclaim a coming storm, and it roared for several days in the aftermath of a storm, which meant that it roared most days, sounding for all the world like a continuous crossing of transatlantic jet liners in the skies overhead.

Relieved for the moment from the tension of negotiating the lake in the dark, we became almost offhand in our pleas to Paud Ruane to finish the wiring to the standards demanded by the ESB. Perversely, that approach succeeded. Suddenly, Paud declared his availability, nay, his absolute determination: "to clear up the shaggin' job". Disconcerted, I consulted Milady. She pointed out that the approach of Christmas might well have a bearing on this elusive artisan's desire to receive payment for work done, even if that meant completing his contract.

Once again Paud demonstrated his liking for having "the run of the place". Every door and every window was thrust ajar, while coils of cable snaked like living things the length and breadth of our windswept house. What could it all be about? Piece by grudging piece the story was divulged. Paud had wired the house to a standard sufficient for the generator, taking the view that my procrastination would never see the ESB on the island. Wrong-footed on that score, he was now faced with "making good", which involved earthing every pipe and every tap and taking these earth wires back to the main fusebox in the kitchen. It was almost as big a task as the initial installation had been and put me in mind of an oft-quoted adage of a Tullamore neighbour years ago: "A job done twice is a job done right!"

The plumbing throughout the old house now bristled with

glaring metal tags bearing the words: "Electrical safety device. Do not remove". How, I enquired nervously, had we survived all those months without these contraptions? "Ah, sure, it's only a load of oul nonsense. They think ye'd be fried in yer baath. 'Tis only makin' work for poor tormented souls like meself. Wasn't th'electric in places for years and years and divil the one ever got killed off of it. An' I wouldn't mind, but now THEY want ME to write YOU a shaggin' cert to say the job's done RIGHT! Sure, what other way would it be done? They have us all gone mad with their bits of paper for this and bits of paper for that and the shaggin' taxman tellin' me I'm a shaggin' MILLIONAIRE!"

By the light of his ex-London Gas Board van, Paud ploughed his biro through that all-important certificate of completion to the safety standards demanded by the ESB. "And that's it now, Paud?"

"As sure as God made little apples! Once they get a smell o' dis in Clifden, they'll be out here before yous can say 'Jumping Jack Flash'!" I couldn't help wincing at the imagery, picturing the vast old iron bath in which you can lie full length. It didn't bear thinking about.

With "proper electricity" now a virtual reality, we could contemplate other aspects of what had become a single-minded existence. Heather Island needed trees, not so much in the immediate vicinity of the house, but down the eastern end, where only bracken and heather and frochans grew. Batman knew just the man for the job: "You might even get a GRANT". So deeply ingrained has the culture of grant-aid become, in what the EC has determined as "Deprived Areas", it almost goes without saying that every action is influenced to an enormous extent by its eligibility for grant aid. In this instance the area to be planted was hardly worth the effort of filling in the grant application; or was that heresy?

Batman duly produced "just the man", a solemn-faced

official from the Forestry Department, exiled some years previously from the comforts of our capital city to the wilds of Castlebar. His demeanour suggested that his conversion to "life in the sticks" might never become total. Mr. Foyle duly carried out his inspection of the site, pronouncing the terrain less than ideal for the cultivation of trees. This was no more or less than I had expected, for journeys across lakes in small boats do seem to disconcert the majority of his ilk. However, his ultimate verdict, "I'll pass you for sycamores, or Christmas trees, if you prefer", came as a blow. So much for my visions of delightful blends of native Irish trees; beech, holly, rowan, hazel, chestnut, hornbeam and perhaps even wild cherry. Unavailingly, I pointed out the exquisite copper beeches growing closer to the house, the ash, the rowans and the holly. Their very existence in this place, according to Mr. Foyle, was an aberration. They had no business being here at all, at all.

Batman could scarcely conceal a smirk. Heather Island might have a half-decent species of bat, but it was faring badly in the social scale of tree types. Sycamore had traditionally been regarded as little better than a weed, until the French began paying exorbitant prices for particular sycamores, the ones with the "rippled" grain. The wood from these trees was in great demand for veneer in cabinet making and was fetching hundreds of pounds per bole, depending on the length and breadth from root to first branch. As to how one could discern these "rippled" trunks from their less gifted fellows ... that was a knack as rare as chicken sexing! Duly, the Department of Agriculture, Food and Forestry confirmed Mr. Foyle's sanction for 1500 three-year-old sycamore saplings, to be planted two metres apart over an area of 0.6 hectares. These should be planted in February, all things being equal. The letter from the Department was succinct: "You should note, however, that the responsibility for the ultimate success of the plantation rests with you."

Well, the fortunes of Heather Island and its beleaguered inhabitants were not to be made from forestry. That was abundantly clear. Could the lake itself be made to contribute to the exchequer? On this we had no shortage of advice. Some said we should stock it with rainbow trout and commercialise the fishing, on a "put and take" basis. The more traditionally minded averred that it would be sacrilegious to introduce that "foreign" species into an old-established brown trout fishery. "What you should do is get on to the hatchery in Cong and see if they could let you have some decent-sized 'stockies'. Put them in at the beginning of next season and keep an eye on what your angling clients catch." That sounded a more agreeable way of reviving our jaded fishery than introducing rainbows, which do not reproduce in Irish waters. As for the sea trout experiment … it would be months before any decision would be reached on that project.

The Western Region Fisheries' hatchery on the outskirts of Cong breeds and rears stock fish for all the great lakes of the west, Corrib, Mask, Carra and Conn, holding up to 200,000 young fish in artificial ponds alongside the river bank. Frank Reilly, the helpful, enthusiastic manager, openly admitted his personal preference for rainbow fishing, declaring that he would travel Ireland for guaranteed rainbow fishing. I began to waver in the face of his missionary fervour. Brownies or rainbows? Was the country full of these closet fanatics, prepared to wade through fire, walk on broken glass, swim swollen rivers to throw a fly over those big, greedy rainbows? Frank's fishy stories suddenly made the denizens of our acid lake seem very small fry indeed.

> Oh God grant me a fish so big that I
> When boasting of it may never need to lie!

Stopping off for one — or three — on our way home, we met

Malcolm, whose attitude to creatures finny is quite free of Waltonian traits. "Come in here," growled Malcolm, turning my path from the bar to the shop and leading me, nonplussed, to the cold cabinet, where the depleted range of winter fish was laid out on display. "Do you see what this bandit is charging for rainbow trout!" I did. £3.85 per pound.

"So?"

"So this, dork. Get yourself a cage. Put it in your lake, somewhere in the lee of the island. Fill it with rainbows. Feed the buggers till they reach three pounds weight and flog them to all the hotels and restaurants. Why should this character get every last penny of everyone's money?"

Maybe Malcolm was right. Instead of drifting aimlessly around the lake, on the whim of the wind, casting three little flies over disinterested, unresponsive little brownies and being happy to take a tenner from other like-minded optimists, why not go overtly commercial? Malcolm's attitude to angling is akin to Oscar Wilde's on foxhunting. Whereas Wilde referred to "The unspeakable in full pursuit of the uneatable", Malcolm views angling as the insane in pursuit of the uncatchable. But fish in cages, regularly fed on high-protein pellets, which they happily convert into succulent, nourishing flesh to titillate the palates of the rich and the famous, and anyone else who can afford it … that makes sense!

And if the rainbows should escape? "Even better! They'll gobble up all your miserable little brownies. Only the bigger brownies will survive. Then you'll have decent fishing to offer. The time they got loose in Lough Fee, one of the rainbows grew to 30 lbs. A monster, he was. A bloody monster!"

Milady contained her feelings until safely in the sanctuary of the Old Schoolhouse, curtains drawn, fire lit, dinner in the oven and a drink in her hand. "If you think, for one moment, that I'm going to live in the middle of a FISH FARM, you've got another think coming! And don't mind that Malcolm. He's been too long in Connemara. It's got to him. He's flipped. Any more of that nonsense and I'll see to it that you get a PROPER JOB again. And it won't be anywhere near this FUNNY FARM. They're all stark, staring MAD down here! What's happened to the smart young marketing executive I married?"

For the first time in years I began to look forward to Christmas. The girls would be home, along with the twins. Milady would be in her element. She loves Christmas, with all its fuss and flap, and people around. And maybe, just maybe, by then I'd have my study fitted out and could hide away in there, cocooned by my beloved books.

December

D ecember kicked off on a distinctly unfestive note. The Garda Síochána announced an all-out onslaught on drinking and driving, with dire consequences for transgressors. The rural outcry was anguished. The very fabric of rural society was threatened, as the media painted harrowing pictures of bachelor farmers confined to their isolated fastnesses, terrified to venture to their local hostelries—their only point of social contact. Dublin publicans predicted mass lay-offs of staff, total collapse of pub values and the imminent insolvency of the national exchequer, through decimated Customs & Excise revenue.

This national emergency was deemed unlikely to affect Letterfrack, with its skeleton bus service and virtual absence of taxis, where the only means of getting to the pub is by car. It could never happen here. The first roadblock erected in the village at dusk caused consternation. However, its felicitous situation—right on the crossroads—enabled all local motorists to approach one of the three pubs with impunity, and there remain until the menace had been removed. Thus were Letterfrack publicans enabled to play their crucial part in maintaining turnover, thereby preventing the collapse of Ireland's exchequer. This spirit of playing one's part in the country's salvation quickly communicated itself to the patrons, who downed their pints with an even greater sense of purpose than usual, spurred to heroic efforts by daily reports of doom and disaster emanating from Dublin, where off-licence sales had soared.

This new-found sense of purpose manifested itself in others ways as well. If Heather Island was to host its first Christmas for over fifty years, much remained to be accomplished to complete the transformation from house to "home". While Milady transformed her kitchen from grimly functional to "designer chic", I secured the services of a gifted handyman to create my shelf-lined study-cum-hideaway, with books from floor to ceiling. Facing south, with three external walls, it had always been the dampest room in the house and thus far from ideal for books. However, I was assured that the lining of the crumbling walls, secured by batons and insulation and an inner shield of tongued-and-grooved cladding would repel the worst of winter's damp. Within days the transformation was complete and my heart's desire fulfilled—a room full of tier upon tier of books, assembled over a long number of years and now readily to hand for the first time ever.

With my desk in front of the south-facing window I could keep half an eye on the lake, in what was steadily becoming a subliminal surveillance of weather conditions. In anything less than gale conditions, a steady blow is manageable when getting back and forth across Tully Lake. It's the squalls that spell danger. Even though sometimes of only ten or fifteen seconds' duration, their sheer ferocity can capsize a boat, while the longer ones can blow you so far off course that rocks become an additional hazard. If the boat is dashed upon a rock broadside to the wind, she is equally liable to capsize.

This new-found sensitivity to the vagaries of the winds enabled me to respond immediately to Milady's queries on the possibility of getting across the lake.

One day, inevitably, I got it wrong. That morning's "gust pattern" appeared to be one of brief, but very violent flurries, separated by five-minute intervals; long enough to traverse the most exposed section in the middle, unsheltered by island or mainland. We were right in the middle when this freak tornado struck, forcing me to turn the bows into the gale and row furiously just to keep in position, waiting for it to pass over. It didn't. Inexorably, we were blown closer and closer to the rocky shore. Between us and dry land lay reefs of submerged rocks. If we met them on the crest of a wave we would be swept cleanly over them, but if we encountered them while in a trough … Somehow, we got through, secured the tossing boat fore and aft and trudged disconsolately towards the boathouse. It was a miserable, demoralising moment, for now I had to swallow the unpalatable truth. I might continue to brave the elements, but I couldn't be sure of besting them.

Bernice in the shop was scathing of our bedraggled plight. "Sure you've no sense," she snapped at me, "expectin' a woman to stop in that place in winter. And you with not even an engine on your currach. Foolin' around with only paddles. Plain stupidity. Men. Not fit to be let out!" Braver than me leave the last word to Bernice, wisely. Foolhardy to point out that more have perished through relying on outboard engines in recent decades than ever were lost using oars, or "paddles" as they call them around here. The oarsman is in the centre of the boat and can use his oars as stabilisers, to a degree.

In contrast, the outboard operator is in the stern, his weight hoisting the bow high out of the water, prey to being buffeted by the winds, even to the extent of the boat being upended altogether. Engines have their uses, on small boats, but not on storm-tossed waters in the depths of winter. Having humiliated me, the elements then proceeded to add insult to injury. Within half an hour the lake was like a millpond, allowing me to retrieve the boat and row it into the safety of the harbour.

As the weather grew progressively worse, Milady became daily more anxious about celebrating Christmas on the island, with good reason. And I could not take issue with her on this one, for the constant dicing with the elements had begun to get to me as well. Each time I reached for a life jacket from the back of the hall door I could feel my heart starting to race. Then down to the boatslip, survey the scene, launch the boat and manoeuvre into position just in the lee of the island, waiting for that all-important "window" in the weather to make a dash for the shore, never knowing what awaited my return. If the Old Schoolhouse was to be the venue, then that was all right by me.

The children were dismayed at this display of parental funk. From Hongkong, from Leicester, from Thurles and Murroe, the response was adamant, "We want Christmas on the island!" Torn between gratitude for their vote of confidence and fear of failure to repay it, I simply prayed that the weather gods would relent, for those few days anyway. Meanwhile, the ESB operatives demonstrated an acute awareness of weather forecasts. They would not be risking life and limb to make the final transfer from generator to mains until the met. office amended their current recitation: "There is a further warning of gales on all Irish coastal waters and on the Irish Sea, with winds gusting up to eighty miles per hour." "Yes," the Clifden depot conceded, "It's a simple enough job for the engineer. But he's the only one we've got and we can't have him gettin' drownded. Not over the Christmas, anyhow!"

Most of that month the elements laid siege to us, until even Bernice conceded that this was the worst December for wind that she could recall. "Day after bloomin' day. And you might think you're bad. If you knew where I live ... 'Tisn't safe to open the door, for fear you'd be blown over to Boston!" Mischievous, unbidden, this image sprang to mind of Bernice as Mary Poppins, suspended from an umbrella, being wafted out over Inisturk, to disappear amidst the scudding clouds over the grey, seething Atlantic ... But on whom would I then depend for my daily debunking of romantic Connemara in winter?

"But Mary Poppins's eyes were fixed on him, and Michael suddenly discovered that you could not look at Mary Poppins and disobey her. There was something strange and extraordinary about her—something that was frightening and at the same time most exciting." P. L. Travers's fantastical nanny had arrived on the wind and left on the wind, and the wind was ever in my mind as Christmas approached. The Mary Poppins analogy was easily explained. When sorting through boxes and boxes of books to try to arrange them in an order that I, at least, could follow, I had come across a first edition, with this inscription: "To Oliver St. John Gogarty for his grandchildren and descendants, from the Author." The dedication was dated 1935.

My grandfather was also in my thoughts, for a variety of reasons. Caught one evening by yet another storm, we had been held captive on the island, where I had spent the time drafting the first Gogarty Society Newsletter, as the generator-driven radio announced that 100,000 homes were without electricity as a result of storm damage. That night we were not alone in the master bedroom. The following morning's post-storm tour of inspection revealed that the only casualty had been one of the five branches from "The Plum Tree By The House", a damson tree outside the bedroom window that had inspired Gogarty's poem of that name.

The events of the previous night found no echoes in such lines from the "Plum Tree" poem as:

> "In morning light my damson showed
> Its airy branches oversnowed
> On all their quickening fronds,
> That tingled where the early sun
> Was flowing soft as silence on
> Palm trees by coral ponds."

Much closer in my thoughts was a verse from another of his poems — "Connemara":

> "You must not ask what kind of light
> Was in the valleys half the night,
> Now that you are beyond Beyonds
> Where night and day were tied by bonds."

The "light" in this instance had been high up on the beamed ceiling, well above any angle of illumination from the curtained windows, mostly purples, mauves and fuchsias, in a murky background. As this kaleidoscope settled and became clearer, I could make out an old-fashioned pub scene, filled with elderly men in topcoats circulating between the partitioned sections of the long counter. I only became frightened when one of these anonymous figures detached himself from the crowd and made as if to draw me into the company. Growing to lifesize as he neared the foot of the bed, he became recognizable: not as the elderly man that I remembered from my childhood, but as that saturnine, sinister portrait by Augustus John. I freaked.

Milady, startled, claimed to see nothing, dived under the bedclothes and told me to do likewise. The main figure rejoined the company, visible even through the covers. Gradually the scene faded, though the suffused lights continued to flicker. After what seemed an age, I plucked up the courage to light the bedside candle. It burned steadily, though shafts of light continued to criss-cross the opposite wall and ceiling, for all the world like anti-aircraft searchlights. Only with the eventual coming of the dawn did these, too, fade and disappear.

What significance should I attach to this lantern show, I wondered; writing it all down, while it remained vividly in mind. Apparitions had been reported in this house over the years, notably in the short passageway between the master bedroom and the bathroom, where, I had to admit, I had often felt ever so slightly ill-at-ease, alone, in the dark of night, with only a lamp or candle for comfort. Over twenty years ago our eldest daughter, then very young, had quizzed her mother about the man who had traversed the veranda, before vanishing through an unopened door. Though she hardly knew him—and definitely not in his island clothes—Monique had described my father. But as he had died in the master bedroom only a couple of weeks earlier, that seemed fair enough. The spirits of the departed do hang around for a while after death. We know that to be so.

This latest manifestation was less easy to work out. Gogarty had died in 1957, almost forty years ago. As far as I knew, he had never reappeared from beyond the grave. So, why should he do so now, and why particularly in a guise that he had always found uncomfortable? His anxiety about that Augustus John picture had inspired the poem, "To My Portrait By Augustus John", of which these are the closing lines:

"Is it a warning? And, to me,
Your criticism upon Life?
If this be caused by Poetry?
What should a Poet tell his wife?
Whate'er it is, howe'er it came,
No matter by what devious track
My image journeyed, there is fame
In that it has come surely back."

Later, in his *Unpremeditated Autobiography*, Gogarty voiced his doubts once more on this sardonic portrait: "If he [Augustus] threw himself into a song it was a promise that he would throw himself into a portrait. Now there are artists whose selves I would not like to have painting me ... With Augustus it is different. His would be a personality to have in your portrait.

"I know you will sense the fact that I look upon portraits as stamping grounds whereupon the painter may dance … After this you will say that I have been impressed by someone's statement to the effect that artists, like children, paint themselves. And you will be right.

"But what of the savage portraits he paints, such as those of Lady Ottoline Morrell and David Lloyd George? Exactly. he knew the rascality of Lloyd George, the schemer, the double-crosser and rogue that he was. It is all there in that unscrupulous face. Lady Ottoline, in his opinion, stood for false values and they are the humps on her breast and back."

Why had Gogarty—that man of many masks—chosen his least favourite image when manifesting himself to me? Was it an omen, a warning of some sort? In the chilly light of that December day I called myself a coward for not braving it out, not seeing it through. But then I persuaded myself that Life is for living and best got on with. Later still, some lines of Swinburne—Gogarty's favourite poet—offered solace of a sort:

> "From too much love of living,
> From hope and fear set free,
> We thank with brief thanksgiving
> Whatever gods may be
> That no man lives forever,
> That dead men rise up never;
> That even the weariest river
> Winds somewhere safe to sea."

Other spectres quickly took their place on our embattled horizon; not least the awful business of "the Christmas shopping". Milady had, in the way of her kind, done her purchasing of offerings over the preceding weeks—if not months. Her smugness on that score only served to increase my desperation. All I had managed to decide upon was a shotgun for Nicholas, even if that meant a trip to Dublin. It did. The advice offered by Watts Bros. on the quays was worth at least as much as the gun: "Might I suggest a single-barrel twenty-bore, Sir? That way you know that when the young man has fired once his gun is then safe. It eliminates that temptation to have another go, which has led to tragedy, more than once ..."

Buoyant upon borrowed wisdom, I found the remainder of my present-buying fell easily into place; too easily as it would transpire. But that pitfall awaits all males, at Christmas time. Doesn't it? Besides, it was an opportunity to commiserate with our less fortunate brethren, doomed to existence in and around the capital, where the breathalyser campaign was causing so much misery, we had heard. Strangely, access to Doheny & Nesbitt's — that celebrated School of Economics — was only achieved after a determined struggle, so great was the press of exuberant imbibers. Had we been misled by those doom-laden media reports of a city on its knees? So it appeared. What a relief our news would be to the valiant imbibers of Letterfrack, threatened with imminent cirrhosis in their role as saviours of the nation's exchequer.

The coming together of our family for this first Christmas on Heather Island was not without mishap. The twins had it easy; by bus and train to Galway, there to be collected and driven out into exterior darkness. The storms seemed to have abated, at least in the west. Rebecca spent a day and a night in dismal Holyhead; proof, if it were needed, that Stena Sealink confuse the Irish Sea with the Serpentine when purchasing ferries. Alannah got from Hongkong to the outskirts of Clifden with little difficulty. But there the omnibus "left the road", and the driver left the bus. Trudging into Clifden, Alannah managed to persuade the only available taxi driver to take her the remaining twelve miles to the shores of Tully Lake. It was a fare he is unlikely to forget, as our avenue claimed yet another exhaust system on his departure. We were now complete, save for Monique, who had her restaurant to run and her in-laws to entertain. We would see her for New Year's Eve, and the party.

This "party" appeared to be an integral part of Milady's "borrowing" of the Old Schoolhouse. At least it wouldn't involve crossing the lake, even in our brand new boat. What a beauty she was; battleship grey hull, gunwale and interior brightly stained and varnished, larch and oak, copper gleaming. Her maker had seemed sad parting with her, artist that he is. Do artists fall in love with their creations? Of course they do; anything less makes them simply artisans. That our new boat was "lucky" became immediately obvious. Her first passenger was Santa Claus, the ESB engineer! To have light at the flick of a switch, and in silence, was all the Christmas present I could desire. How well the Christmas tree looked under its robe of fairy lights. As for the sheer elation on being freed from the tyranny of that generator … Had we at last achieved that transformation from house to home? It felt that way. Yes, it did!

Our prayers for calm weather throughout Christmas answered so far, we had decided against venturing out to Midnight Mass, opting instead for a leisurely dinner en famille. Christmas Eve dinner is always roast ham. Milady had adhered to that practice even in Macau. As we sat in the drawingroom, chatting about Christmases past, in Tullamore, in Yorkshire and Macau, and the final realisation of that oft-mooted notion—Christmas on the island—we did so beneath the gaze of the Gogarty children, whose portrait hangs above the fireplace. Rescued from the burning of Renvyle House in 1923, it had been restored and had now returned to Connemara, where it had been painted in 1916. Dermot and Noll are pictured either side of my mother, a girl of five at that time. Noll, the eldest, lived in retirement in Dublin. My mother had died some years ago, as had Dermot a decade previously.

I had never met my uncle Dermot, the oarsman, draughtsman, RAF pilot and post-war manager of Renvyle House Hotel, for he had lived abroad throughout his latter years. Among the family papers one poem of Dermot's has survived, appropriate to this occasion.

CONNEMARA CHRISTMAS
The towering clouds from off the western sea
Speed heavy-uddered to the Plains of Meath.
To pass as shadows o'er the fertile lea
And leave the bog and cabin dry beneath.

Twelve jagged Pins tear ope the laden skies,
Till milk-white torrents scar their heathered flanks.
To fill the Loughs with many coloured dyes,
Where gentle winds form meerschaum on their banks.

The failing light, the coming night portends,
Dark Eve embraces distant Tullybaun
And rising steals the colour from the Bens.
The Sons of Conn await the Coming Dawn.

Before the Heavens can acclaim their place,
Each cabin window shows a vigil light.
The Earth and Sky compete in boundless peace,
To welcome travellers on this Holy Night.

Christmas Day was all that any of us could wish. Following late Mass, friends came over for drinks across a lake that sported scarcely a ripple, marvelling at this lull, after weeks of rain and gales. This once, anyway, the womenfolk didn't dress as lumberjacks, displaying instead an elegance and femininity that I found both startling and stimulating, after half a year in

Connemara, eyes anaesthetised by dreary denim.

Later that day the lake became a mirror, reflecting in its surface the surrounding hillsides and the "great rock" that is Letter Hill. The only ripples were caused by aimless mallard, cruising swans and the children, as they boated, carefree in the calm. "A man travels the world over in search of what he needs, and returns home to find it." — George Moore, homo sapiens.

Christmas Day in Connemara is, literally, a ceasefire for sportsmen. St. Stephen's Day sees hostilities resumed, with gusto. Nicholas didn't believe we would ever get to the clay pigeon range at Halfway House, over the Mayo border on the Westport road. He acquitted himself well, excelling on the "Springing Teal" and doing passably on the "Cock 'n Hen". Camellia, wary of being bruised by the recoil, eventually consented to have a go at the "Running Rabbit", under the tutelage of Phelim O'Flaherty. Having scored one "kill" from her solitary shot, she retired in triumph, to her brother's chagrin.

The older girls, whose time in Connemara was limited, accompanied their mother to walk the dogs on the broad expanses of deserted Glassilaun beach, where Plover plunged boisterously into the ocean, while Teal barked at the elegant oystercatchers and wheeling gulls that hovered tantalisingly out of reach, just above the waves. Delightful in summer, Glassilaun is mind-blowing in winter, when its very emptiness becomes awe-inspiring, combining earth and sea and sky to make you feel so small amid the vastness of such surroundings.

The woodcock were in, though on the higher slopes, the weather being clement. But the snipe were plentiful on the lower bogs, their location influenced by the phases of the moon. Would Nicholas care to try? Would fish swim! "And can we bring Teal? Please!" Young though she was, she was said to have done some work with her mother. We'd chance her, but on her own, without the trundling Plover, whose only idea was to play. We'd walk Greenmount bog, in behind the church in Tullycross and Teal must work to Nicholas, whose gundog she was. Hopelessly exuberant initially, she put up snipe miles out of range.

However, as the afternoon wore on, Teal steadied, working closer to her youthful master. Eventually, she set a snipe, just the other side of a drain. Nicholas crossed and motioned Teal to follow. As though she had been doing this for years, the bitch sprang noiselessly across, and set again. Gun at the ready, Nicholas signalled her to flush his quarry. He waited, gave the snipe its chance, and fired. Yes! His first snipe, at his first attempt too! But for Teal, we could still be searching the heather for that snipe, which she located, but would not retrieve, as dusk came down. It had been quite a day for one young man and his dog.

One small snipe does not dinner make ... Would we ask Alastair to stuff and mount it? "Oh, smart one, Dad! Alastair's sound out." We drove up to Rosleague Manor, that country house hotel where Alastair acts as head chef during the summer season. To while away the long winter evenings he had taken up taxidermy, teaching himself through specialist videos. So far he had completed a fox and a Great Northern Diver.

The snipe looked tricky at this early stage in his new-found career. "OK, I'll have a go. You haven't forgotten you're minding 'Cedar' while I'm away, have you?" Cedar is Alastair's tall, loping German pointer and constant companion. "Of course not. Just say when, and drop him over." The island was the perfect repository for this good gundog that had a tendency to roam when idle, in a countryside thickly populated with sheep ...

All too soon New Year's Eve was upon us. Amid fluster and flurry the Old Schoolhouse was declared ready, for "party time". It was to be a two-phase party, the organisers agreed. For tradition dictated that the Old Year must be sent on its way and the New Year welcomed in by dancing at the crossroads in Letterfrack. Therefore Phase One would include a buffet in the Old Schoolhouse, to which all those involved living locally would contribute dishes. The menfolk had taken care that no shortage of drink would bring the festivities to a premature close. Towards the witching hour the revellers would adjourn to the hostelries of their choice in Letterfrack, converging in a gigantic circle on the crossroads for Auld Lang Sygne. The scene would then revert to the Old Schoolhouse, where only the fittest could hope to survive.

When Connemara fills with visitors for Christmas, it does so almost surreptitiously, the intake being absorbed by friends and relations living here. New Year's brings an entirely different invasion, thronging the hotels, jamming the pubs. It is as though there is a mass migration from homes throughout Ireland, and even further afield, domestic duties discharged once Christmas is over. It's fun! We were joined by Monique, her husband, Bill, and our grandson, Samuel. And thus—albeit briefly—we were together as a family for the first time since I had departed Yorkshire for Macau almost two years before.

We were also joined by Brian and Suzanne, friends from Tullamore and an interesting contrast in terms of our respective life cycles. Though of an age with ourselves, Brian and Suzanne represented the in-between generation. Their children had left the nest and their parents were all still living. Milady and I, "orphaned" for several years now, were still some way away from the "empty nest" syndrome. It was something that struck us during our years in North Yorkshire; the number of our married contemporaries with complete sets of parents still hale and hearty. Intimations of mortality are deferred until that preceding generation suffers its first fatality, breaking that united front. Milady and I had been fatherless for over twenty years; motherless for five. I mention this merely because being projected to the front of the queue on the divingboard of Life does alter one's perceptions; like it or not.

Is it the recollection of the demise of a year that makes one somewhat maudlin? I think it is. This notion of, "Off with the old! On with the new!", as though forcibly deprived of favourite old garments, familiar, friendly, reassuring; far from sure that their pristine replacements may not prove an awkward fit, pinching in places, itchy in others. It may also be that whole tempo of life in Connemara, totally removed from the traumas of everyday urban struggle for survival, makes one reluctant to let go of an existence that is sheer enjoyment in itself. It is the ultimate "Land of time enough". Hustle and bustle, confrontation and frustration, I need go no further than Dublin to find. Renvyle House Hotel appropriated the sub-title "Ireland's only stress free zone", with significant success, if conversational response is any guide.

Once again the weather held. It seemed we had but barely managed to get a drink in the crowded pub when the cry went up: "To the cross, everybody!" From all three pubs they streamed out, momentarily blinded by the plunge from light to darkness, shuffling into an enormous circle, arms crossed, wrists grasped to withstand the surging to and fro to the time-honoured refrain.

As he has done for years now, portly Simon McCormick led this motley choir into the opening bars. "For the sake of Auld Land Syne ..." he boomed. But Simon's well-oiled baritone was obliterated by a dreadful, discordant cacophony of sound from two hundred throats or more, the task of moving in and out in any sort of harmony, and singing in tune, and remembering to refill deflated lungs proving beyond the powers of all but the few.

This ritual complete, the tired and the emotional repaired in search of restoratives, while our party returned to the Old Schoolhouse to embark on Phase Two—the endurance test. It was as though no interruption had occurred. In moments the place was heaving. The choice of music mattered little, for Kraken had entered his trumpet phase, in which he repeats the same refrain, sporadically and with scant concession to the music he purports to "accompany, yah!"

As this marathon ground on, tactical withdrawal became the order of the day. We had enough beds. It just seemed a good move to occupy them before others thought better of taking to the roads and pre-empted our stealthy retreat. At first it seemed preferable that the ladies should retire, thus securing berths for their menfolk. This eminently sound suggestion evoked the startling rejoinder that the men might set an example, marking the dawn of a New Year, and all that. Consternation! When these "discussions" begin it is time to take unilateral action.

In those few moments between my boarding "feather island" and succumbing to slumber, the past six months replayed themselves, video-style. Macau; those 4.00 a.m. forays across the arching Taipa Bridge to the racecourse, where exercise must finish before 7.00 and the onslaught of searing sunshine. Tennis and swimming and beers in the shade by the sailing club, and the constant sensation of life passing by in suspended animation. Going through the motions, albeit well-paid, but to what end? My reckless response. Go back. Make a home. Make a life. From what?

The shambles that was Heather Island and its toppling house. The pulling and the dragging to turn desolation into an abode where family and friends could come and go and fashion their own lives. Where we could make a nest; put down roots in ancestral lands, give the twins a sense of place, of identity, of belonging. The older girls, though scattered now, had grown up between two fixed points—Tullamore, and the island in summer. The twins deserved no less.

The old house had been made habitable, I thought. It might lack a few mod. cons., but that was merely a function of money.

All-year-round access was a bigger issue, and one that I hadn't really made much progress towards resolving. It remained the biggest bogey, to me anyway. Access was the stumbling block to any way of making Heather Island pay, that involving transferring people to and fro. Maybe writing was the answer. Look at "Hemingway" after all.

Milady had her job, which could develop into other fields. Hadn't she spoken of concert programmes in her beloved Gothic chapel? And as for me? The honeymoon that had been the putting together of Heather Island was coming to an end. Sadly. But the purse had become very light and needed refilling. That looked like becoming Priority Number One. The family business was in the throes of being sold and that would help. But it was still not what they call "bankable". Could I write for a living? There! That was the solution.

With that the tape ran out, the video machine that spun those issues past my inner vision shut down and I was asleep, insensible to trumpet blasts, be they Kraken's or the angels'.

January

⇛

T hey stood not on the order of their going, but went at once—to Hongkong, Leicester and Kildare—did our daughters. I felt for Milady, moving mountains to assemble her brood, only to lose them after such a short time together. It seemed to heighten her sense of isolation, in the wintry wastes of Connemara, all too far from the maddin' crowd. But the twins were not yet due to depart and we had Vincent's newly acquired "sporting estate" to inspect— Prospect House, Killadangan, Westport, in the foothills of Croaghpatrick, Ireland's sacred mountain.

Vincent and I had soldiered together years before, in Tullamore, when he represented Irish Mist all over the globe and I imported wines and spirits for the domestic market. In between trips abroad we had fished and shot and played squash together, kindred souls displaced in the sleepy Irish midlands. Since then he had climbed the executive totem pole in London. Prospect House, with two hundred acres and two little lakes, was ample evidence of his success. We brought our dogs and the visiting Cedar, for a home base in the Fulham Road doesn't lend itself to the keeping of gundogs, if one has any feeling for them.

Nicholas and I, Vincent Sr. and Vincent Jr., (near enough Nicholas's age), spent the day flushing pheasants and mallard—to no avail—for we had not got the lie of the land, with its hills and its hollows. It was only towards dusk that we

106

stumbled on a cache of woodcock in the "badlands" at the western extremity. And you need the best of winter light to hit those wily, feinting "fairy" birds. It was, we agreed over a bottle before a blazing fire, a fabulous setting for a driven pheasant shoot, with potential for half a dozen different stands. The very terrain, with its precipitous slopes and high trees would always cause problems for one man and his dog. No matter, the two boys could learn their rough shooting with me in Connemara and the more recherché art of driven pheasant on the slopes above Clew Bay.

Enjoyable as the encounter had been, it left me distinctly uneasy. Vincent had acquired his Irish estate through dint of hard work in London and would pay for it out of earnings. When the time came he would be able to retire to Prospect House and live out his days on his corporate pension. That made sense. And I? I had thrown up a job, a cushy number, renounced what couldn't even be called the rat race and avowed my intention of living in Connemara, with neither income nor pension. That did not make sense, not by a long chalk. Better get going on this writing business ...

In a most timely instance of symbiosis, John Coyle, grand vizier of Galway and patron of the arts, decided to have the history of his Renvyle House Hotel rewritten. What better man to do it! "There, Milady, a commission!" Milady was sceptical. "You'll never get into the mainstream, hiding down here. However, it's a start."

Little did I realise it, but "the mainstream" was closer than I could have guessed ... The twins' return to school was the signal for Milady's winter exodus, this time to a borrowed house in that respectable Dublin suburb, Dundrum. I could come, or I could stay. Simple as that.

The weather gods sided with Milady. Soon after she had issued her ultimatum, I noticed water falling in the "little court paved with irregular slats, russet and brown and sea-green."

Nothing particularly remarkable in that, in Connemara, in January; except that it wasn't raining. Only when we reached the far shore a few minutes later did the truth dawn on me. As I tied up the boat to that great boulder with the iron eye inset, that only one man in Renvyle can lift, I glanced to the west end of the lake. By some trick of the wind, a veil of lakewater, fully two hundred feet high, was being whipped up into the air and carried, like a gigantic stage curtain, the length of the lake. That was how the courtyard was being drenched. "Apocalyptic" was the word that sprang to mind.

Lest I prevaricate, the weather gods rattled their bag of tricks—and covered us in snow. It looked simply splendid on Muilrea, the Maamturks and the Twelve Bens; the Alps coming to Ireland. It wasn't quite as appreciated in the boat, turning the floorboards into a skating rink, moving Milady to bring forward her departure. The gods giggled—and turned the snow to ice. The lake froze, all the way across. By no means thick enough to walk upon, it was sufficient to bring boating to a standstill. There is nothing to match the frustration of trying to row a boat through ice. The blades of the oars skitter uselessly across the frozen surface.

Should you manage to bash holes through which to insert the oars, then the ice lacerates both the shafts of the oars and the bows of the boat. The solution—if you are unwilling to await a thaw—is to have one person in the bow, laying all about him with a weighty pole, while the other inches forward with the oars. It makes for a lengthy crossing, begging the old question: "Is your journey really necessary?" By and large the answer must be "No", though that is to miss the point of the exercise; our freedom to come and go.

"Destination Dundrum" became instead the arctic wastes of the Curragh of Kildare, to baby-sit a racing stable. Not my idea of fun in January, but one favour deserved another, and we could bring the animals. Alastair intervened. Feeding our dogs and cat would give him reason to stir out each day, other than to the pub; a measure perhaps of how quiet things get in the post-Christmas moratorium that Connemara had become. It felt as though the prospect of Christmas and the New Year festivities had only postponed total hibernation. The roads were empty, the pubs subdued and the only movement on the landscape farmers foddering cattle and sheep and the children going to and from school. The emptiness was magnificent, if a little eerie. Captain Cook may have experienced similar sensations stepping ashore on undiscovered territories, not knowing whether the natives were hostile, nor, indeed, if they even existed.

I was not sorry to be relieved of my unsought role as racehorse custodian. Love can die and Life go on. Alastair had removed Teal and Plover to the mainland, leaving supplies out for the anonymous cat. His actions had been prompted by such horrendous gale warnings that he and Donal, the shopkeeper, and Donal's brother Brendan, the butcher, had lifted the boat from the lake and lashed it securely in the lee of the boathouse. They had done us one almighty favour, for the storm had completely wrecked one end of Renvyle House, torn away coastal roads, lifted whole roofs off sheds and scattered roof tiles by the thousand. The countryside looked drained, exhausted. And the island? We made that crossing sick with apprehension, dreading the devastation that must lie in store, all our work undone ... The path was strewn with branches, but the house itself was undamaged, protected by "the great rock of Letter Hill." Our only loss was one we least expected. Of the pair of resident swans, only one remained, and swans are monogamous.

The damage caused by this storm signalled an abrupt end to the general hibernation. The roads were now a riot of vans, trucks, tractors and trailers, all ferrying roofing materials to effect emergency repairs, lest another sudden gale make a bad situation infinitely worse. No more "the land of time enough", this could not be deferred, delayed, postponed or otherwise enveloped in that enchanting but exasperating philosophy — "The Man that made Time made plenty of it … and we'll be a long time dead." It was almost with a sense of shame that I admitted that the island had escaped unscathed. Any mention of the missing swan would have invited a suitably scathing response.

The hustle and bustle and general commotion affected us in another way. Kraken had a live buyer for the Old Schoolhouse and requested vacant possession. How soon could we vacate? "As soon as ever we can find transport!" And so it began once again, loading the contents of one house onto a lorry and shifting a few miles up the road to the boat house, there to await final transfer to the island. Could two be crammed into one? They'd have to be, and, in due course, they were, though some things, inevitably, had to be discarded; pieces that had been carried into the island seventy years before and remained in situ ever since. It seemed almost sacrilegious, carting old, familiar, clapped-out, uncomfortable furnishings, balancing them — naked and forlorn in their unaccustomed exposure — on the gunwales of boats; an act of gross betrayal, a sundering of one's very self.

Another indirect consequence of this unseasonal upheaval was a move to combine the interests of fishery owners in the area and present a united case in search of EU Structural Funding, as it's called. The exploratory meeting would take place in Salruck House, over on the Little Killary, home of retired Canon Willoughby. One doesn't care to venture out at night when approaching one's centenary. It was like stepping back in time, entering that faded elegance of pre-war Wisdens, patterned wallpaper of indeterminate design, framed photographs of long-dead military men, in an atmosphere of gentility that I can recall but could never recreate.

Secluded in woodland overlooking the Little Killary, one of the finest natural harbours in Connemara, Salruck House is the focal point of the Cushkillary estate, passed down through successive marriage alliances since being granted to Robert Miller by Oliver Cromwell. The estate became known as Thomsons' following the marriage of Alexander Thomson to the widowed Anne Miller in 1815. her husband had been killed in the Peninsula War four years previously. It is a measure of the esteem in which the Thomsons were held locally, through Famine times and beyond, that the IRA guaranteed the widowed Marie Louise Thomson immunity from the campaign of arson they were pursuing during the civil war. Canon Willoughby's wife is a great-granddaughter of General Alexander Thomson and came to live in Salruck House following her husband's retirement as Provost of Tuam in 1973.

Insistent upon being helped to his feet to greet each arrival, ninety-nine-year-old Canon Willoughby was subsequently content to give the floor to his visitors, notably to Sr. Benedict, in charge of all matters sporting and agricultural in Kylemore Abbey.

Charming, quietly spoken, this former barrister with a twinkle in her eye described what the Benedictines proposed to do to enhance the fishing on the Kylemore system, before handing over to Mrs. Willoughby and her grandson, John Ormsby, whose responsibility their Culfin system had become. As they discussed smolts and hatcheries, redds and spawning beds, I began to feel distinctly menial, a smallholder among landlords. But I had come to the meeting with Cathal Heanue, whose brainchild it was. Cathal, as he said himself, merely represented the Culfin Anglers' Club—and they owned nothing, at least in the way of fishing waters. Cathal was being modest, for it was almost entirely due to the drive and enthusiasm of his club that this coming together of independent, unorganised interests had occurred. It was eventually resolved, over tea and biscuits, that we would convene as soon as the Central Fisheries Board might indicate the availability of funding, or otherwise ...

Watching television a few nights later, the Willoughbys may have wondered somewhat about the Benedictines' priorities when Mother Abbess stepped forward under the lights of the TV cameras to receive the £30,000 prize under the "Heritage and Environment" category in the AIB Better Ireland awards scheme. Milady was, of course, ecstatic, for the award applied to the recent restoration of her beloved Gothic Chapel. Sr. Benedict was doubtless equally pleased, for the nuns' next project was to restore the eight-acre walled garden laid out by Mitchell Henry, creator of Kylemore Castle, "one of the wonders of the west—a fairy palace in the Connemara highlands."

On occasion we would walk the dogs in the extensive grounds of Kylemore, calling on Sr. Benedict if she should happen to be in the walled gardens. Looking around today it is impossible to visualise them as once they were, when Mitchell Henry had transplanted the entire village of Pollacappul over to better holdings in Lettergesh to make way for his grand design. Today's dilapidation comprised twenty-three greenhouses, heated by three miles of hot water piping. Curvilinear, these glass houses were similar in design to those of the Botanic Gardens in Dublin. Heating was by means of a boiler atop a limekiln below the exterior walls, the burnt lime then being spread as fertiliser. Water and electricity were provided by damming the outflow from a lake eight hundred feet up the mountainside. And all of this was achieved almost 150 years ago, to create Mitchell Henry's "rose blooming in a wilderness".

The Benedictines—in conformity with their motto "Pax"— do not allow shooting over their estate. Not that this is as great a deprivation as it might sound, for the woods are disappointingly devoid of gamebirds, save for the occasional woodcock. These woodcock were plentiful throughout the rest of the Letterfrack Gun Club's territories this winter, becoming a popular pursuit as the season drew to its close at the end of January.

On one particular Sunday we assembled at Alastair's quarters in Rosleague. The shooting party comprised Pat, a farmer, Bob, a builder, Batman, Geoffrey, the angler, Mark, the marine biologist, Alastair and the writer. It was swiftly agreed that the first-named trio would take a broad sweep across Crocnaraw and Moyard, creating one arm of a pincer movement, complemented by the remainder moving up from Dooneen, through Ungwee and Attirowerty to Baunoges, the source of the tumbling Dooneen river. By working up along either side of the ravine, flanked by hazel, alder and clumps of gorse, we could expect to flush the odd pheasant in the lower reaches, then woodcock and, higher still, snipe.

Refining our strategy still further, we split into pairs, one either side of the ravine. Alastair and Geoffrey took Cedar, leaving Mark and myself with Mark's enthusiastic but rough-mouthed springer bitch. Mark explained his philosophy of damage limitation in regard to his gundog. "Jessie mangles every bird she retrieves. But she will only retrieve from water. Won't pick up on dry land. Gives me a sporting chance." Of greater concern, to Mark's way of thinking, was the practice of having two pairs of guns covering ground that lay between them ... Taking his point, I quietly angled myself somewhat further away from the ravine. An enthusiastic slaughterer of game in my time, I get more pleasure nowadays from watching dogs work well. We drew a blank in the pheasant coverts, to Alastair's audible relief, for he had reared them in a pen behind Rosleague prior to their release and thus formed an emotional attachment.

Further up, amid cries of "Cock, cock!" and volleys of shot, success is proclaimed from the far bank; one apiece to Alastair and Geoffrey. Mark—his honour now at stake—wings a woodcock. Jessie rushes in to finish off this flapper. It may prove difficult to carve. Mark explains further: "Jessie won't pick up off dry land, but she'll put them out of their misery!" Teal, I thought to myself, was infinitely better employed walking the grounds of Kylemore with Milady, than taking example from Jessie. By now we had reached the copse at the summit, with the score still standing at two for them, one to us. The copse being more extensive on their side than ours, Alastair and Geoffrey elected to go through it rather than detour. This they announced quite distinctly.

Suddenly the dogs put up a covey of woodcock, winging downstream, thick and fast. Mark fires one shot. His quarry jinks into the copse. He fires again. An anguished howl from within. Alastair has been hit! Happily, it transpired that "hit" merely meant peppered. The woodcock was less fortunate. As invariably happens in these moments of high drama, another woodcock all but took my cap off as he made his escape, sensing—as they do—that I was too distracted to pose any threat.

In normal circumstances we might have retraced our steps downstream, for woodcock seldom fly too far before seeking shelter once more. But Alastair's mishap indicated a change of tactics and terrain. We would walk windswept Baunoges in search of snipe, as a prelude to joining the others. Unspoken, but tacitly understood, was the consideration that Baunoges is devoid of trees, since the conifer plantation was felled last summer. In rough shooting, as opposed to warfare, visibility is a form of insurance.

Hardly had our "drive" commenced when Cedar set a snipe, holding it hypnotised in his gaze until he should be commanded to flush it. It wasn't only because Cedar is Alastair's dog that he was unanimously elected executioner.

The rest of us retired behind the man and his dog. Alastair gave the office. The snipe rose in a trice. Before he could get into that characteristic zig-zag routine a single shot rang out. Cedar dutifully retrieved and we moved on to draw the extensive covert in Roscrea. From Moyard we heard regular fusillades, suggesting that Alastair's wasn't the only snipe to meet his Waterloo on that sunlit Sunday afternoon.

Above us, as we walked towards our next destination, was a constant streel of vapour trails, all heading west across the Atlantic, high over Inisturk and Inisbofin. I couldn't help wondering at the hopes and fears, ambitions and misgivings preoccupying the minds of those Transatlantic passengers, while we strolled in the sunshine far below in simple celebration of country pursuits. The companionable silence suggested that none of us would willingly swop places, not just now anyway.

Roscrea, a steep headland once renowned for its garlic, sports a sizeable gorse thicket, from which birch and alder protrude; ideal for 'cock. We pair off again to cover both the higher and lower sides. Mark and Alastair put their dogs in from the lower side, while Geoffrey and I take up position above. Duly comes the cry, "Cock, cock high!" Swivelling to sight this elusive quarry, I am distracted by Geoffrey's response. He has thrown himself full-length on the grass! Convulsed with laughter, I let another woodcock swish silently by. Time to think of other things, like Opening Time, for it was nearly half past four.

Here was an another instance of great minds thinking alike. Hardly had our first pints settled on the counter when we were joined by Pat and Bob and Batman. Three more black pints swiftly summoned, we compare "bags". They have bettered us, with five woodcock and three snipe. Still and all, 'tisn't bad, we agree, for an afternoon stroll, on the grand day that was in it. Sure, a man could hardly ask for more ... "More? More stout,

115

is it? Geraldine, give us those again, like a good woman!"

As pint followed pint, so the tales got taller and taller. Mark painted a lurid picture of the newly introduced mallard in Screebe sticking their beaks down the barrels of the guns, presumably to get it all over with quickly, to the delight of the overseas "sportsmen", who declared this the epitome of wildfowling. Batman regaled us with stories of his stalking prowess when charged with culling the deer that roamed the National Park. Alastair could not resist it: "If I find any more of your bloody deer munching the camellias in Rosleague, I won't be ringing you to come and cull them!" Batman fell silent. The rangers are justly proud of their success in reintroducing native Irish deer to Connemara. However, their friends with gardens in the vicinity agree that they could be prouder still if they could persuade their dear deers to confine their depredations to the paltry five thousand acres of National Park, that is so expensively fenced.

Sensing his moment, the landlord appeared in our midst, coffee and cigar in hand. "It's sure to be a huge funeral in Clifden tomorrow. That poor man kept many a rogue out of gaol." Those in the know nodded their agreement. James B. Joyce had been a legend in his own lifetime in the courts of Connemara, becoming extremely popular with the judiciary, many of whom he would have briefed on their path to higher office. Of the many, many anecdotes attaching to James B. Joyce's reputation, the landlord enjoyed this one most. It concerned a defendant in a particularly abstruse case, where the truth, in all likelihood, would never emerge, for what is "truth" in such circumstances? Wearying of his client's tortuous tale, riddled with assumptions, suppositions, nuances and innuendo, James B. had cut his man short: "Listen here to me now. You tell me the truth. Leave the lies to me!"

Lies, it was made plain to me at a breakfast briefing in Renvyle House, should find no place my re-write of *A Sea-grey*

House. However, in certain particulars, an economy with the truth might not go amiss. I was mildly surprised to find that my patron had been educated by the Benedictines, assuming this casuistry to be the exclusive preserve of my own mentors, the Jesuits. The original opus had been scripted some years before by the then chef, which doubtless explained the drooling references to the "home-produced Connemara lamb, renowned for its flavour" and "free range hens roaming around the yard, providing fresh farm eggs for the breakfast table." Not only was the social cachet of this historied house to be enhanced, but any undue emphasis on recently departed "characters" should be correspondingly adulterated ... "Do you perhaps get my drift?" I did. I did indeed.

As part of this brief required me to place Renvyle House in the "continuum of human habitation on Renvyle peninsula" since time immemorial, I sought the guidance of Michael Gibbons, Connemara's indigenous archaeologist and natural historian, who had been so very helpful with the Gogarty Society convention. Michael waxes lyrically on the subject of the Renvyle peninsula, describing it as "an archaeological garden". Who better to consult?

Over cups of coffee in Griffin's Bar—the oldest pub in Clifden in one family's ownership—Michael proceeded to give me an outline of 6000 years of human occupation of the Renvyle peninsula, with the caveat that new discoveries were being identified and confirmed almost daily. These included a pre-bog house site in Cloonluane, a portal tomb nearby, a prehistoric house site overlooking Renvyle Hotel itself and of course, Michael's particular favourite, the stone alignment overlooking Tully Lake. From more recent centuries he instanced children's burial grounds, early Christian mass rocks and booley huts. And if I cared to throw in the Church of the Seven Sisters (said to have been the daughters of a British king), Graunuaile's castle, ring forts, dolmens, pre-bog field systems and—not least—the crannóg in Tully Lake, I'd have enough, "to flatten your average Joe Soap!" If it were only so easy. Maeve Binchy graces the Clifden Writers Week each year. her advice is ever the same: "Write about what you know." I promised to enlist on one of Michael's Connemara Walks that he conducts each day throughout the summer, this time with a tape recorder at the ready.

Having made some progress on the pre-history of the peninsula, I was now faced with unravelling the reign of the O'Flaherties, the ruling clan in these parts until eventually overcome, not by Elizabeth, but by Cromwell. On mature reflection I concluded that my predecessor probably knew more on this subject than I was ever likely to unearth, and thus left well alone. The Blakes were easier, if only because their tenure was so thoroughly documented since its commencement in 1689. That brought me to the Gogartys, who purchased Renvyle in 1917, initially as a private house and subsequently as an hotel, which was sold once more in 1952. So far, so good.

My grandfather's books are littered with references to Renvyle House, which answered his quest: "I am looking for the largest house, farthest from the railhead in Ireland, something that may be even two days away, because this afternoon I saw an automobile that will bring that house within half a day's reach in allowing for the lag in human thinking. I want to get it while it is almost unsaleable, while it is still cheap." In purchasing Renvyle, "out of the proceeds of a year's teetotalism", Gogarty "had a house in the heart of Connemara on the edge of the sea on the last shelf of Europe in the next parish to New York."

"Out of the proceeds of a year's teetotalism"; there was something to conjure with. My uncle, in a TV interview for Rupert's television documentary *Silence Would Never Do*, had parried this question, saying that elucidation would imply that his father had been a roaring alcoholic! In truth, those who

knew Gogarty well described him as a moderate drinker, with
a lively imagination and a fondness for ambiguity. The answer
to this riddle had to lie somewhere ...

It did, in the vaults of Arthur Cox & Co., St. Stephen's
Green, Dublin. Arthur Cox, whose nondescript appearance
masked a brilliant legal brain, had acted for Gogarty, until
intimations of his mortality prompted him to join the Jesuits!
His ghost is reputed to haunt the practice that bears his name,
one of the foremost legal firms in Ireland today. A painstaking
search—was there ever any other form of search—through
bales of musty old documents finally yielded the answer. Even
by today's inflationary standards the figure implies a liberality
with the decanter, although the Gogartys did stage literary
salons in Ely Place each Friday.

Closer to home, my search for stories of their Renvyle days
from former Gogarty retainers meant that the word spread
rapidly; "Yer man 'athin on th'island's writin' a book. 'Tis on th'
hotel below!" This was just what the pioneers of the recently
inaugurated community radio—Connemara FM—wanted to
hear. "Maybe you'd review a few books for us? Would Friday
nights be OK? Well, that's great. Will you give us fifteen
minutes on this one? On Friday, half eight. Don't forget now!"
Trapped! What was more, the slim little paperback looked as
though it could be read from cover to cover in fifteen minutes.
How on earth would I find enough to waffle about for a
quarter of an hour? I needn't have worried ...

Entitled *Connemara After The Famine*, this slim volume is sub-
titled "Journal of a Survey of the Martin Estate, 1853", written
by the surveyor, young Glaswegian, Thomas Colville Scott and
published by my erstwhile schoolmate, Anthony Farrell of
Lilliput Press. It proved "unputdownable", for two reasons.
Firstly, it painted a graphic picture of 200,000 acres of
"inhabited desolation"—the consequence of seven years of
famine. Secondly, the candour of Scott's journal charts his

conversion from bumptious little disparager of all things Irish to champion of an oppressed population that sought only the opportunity to better itself, if such could be attained. His conversion was swift, to judge from the following excerpts.

On his journey by train from Dublin to Galway, Scott observed: "At several intermediate stations on this line, I witnessed emigrants taking their departure for America, by Dublin and Liverpool. These partings are affecting to those who witness them for the first time, but they soon become ludicrous, from their boisterous grief and wailings, especially when we see two unshaven greybearded men, hugging and kissing each other, until as much friction is produced by the contact of their chins, as would result from that of two friendly New Zealanders' noses."

Two days later, Scott has commenced his survey on behalf of the Martin family's mortgagers, the London Law Life Insurance Society: "In going and returning from Roundstone, I looked at many of the rude graves in the Bogs, Quarry holes and even on the ditches, into which the unfortunate people were flung in the time of the famine of '47. The very dogs which had lost their masters or were driven by want from their homes, became roving denizens of this district & lived on the unburied or partially buried corpses of their late owners and others, and there was no possible help for it, as all were prostrate alike, the territory so extensive, and the people so secluded and unknown. The luxuriant tufts of grass and heath shew the spots where they lie."

Before that snowy week in February was out, Scott's conversion was complete: "Walked around 10 miles of the coast, inspecting nine isolated Lots on the way. One called 'Aughrusbeg', has a good house upon it, and is in a fine position for fishing and seaweed: but it is covered with unrecognized subtenants who pay to the middleman double his entire rent.

"I saw these subtenants at work, most of them widows,

forsaken wives; and young women, carrying peat on their backs. They were nearly in a state of nudity, and appeared from actual want, to be almost reduced to a state of Idiocy. There is no Irish animation and buoyancy here, but a stealthy and timid look, as if these poor souls were ashamed of their condition, and lost to the faintest hope of escape from wretchedness and misery. Good God! Where are their landlords & the responsible power that rules over them: have they never looked into these all but vacant faces only animated with a faint imploring look—have they never seen the bent back of the aged, and the sunk cheek of the young? then let them come here and see what neglect has done."

Those are comparatively mild extracts from a startling firsthand account of the greatest calamity ever to strike Connemara. Scott's journal contains many infinitely more harrowing descriptions of his findings. But whether I would be advised to quote from such a book over the airwaves, in the very area that Scott described ... My Jesuit education came to the rescue. I underlined certain passages, and invited my interviewer to read them in her cuddly Liverpudlian tones, while I waffled on about the symbiosis of this unpublished journal having been discovered in an English auction rooms by antiquarian bookdealer Neville Figgis, who happens to have his summer house in nearby Ross.

Mention of this sleight of hand to Mat brought forth his Jesuit yarn, which was set in the house he now occupies, formerly the home of Sir Horace Plunkett, pioneer of the cooperative movement in Ireland. On the eve of a critically important luncheon in Kilteragh, at which Sir Horace planned to advance the cause of peace between the Provisional Government and the British Cabinet, his indispensable housekeeper discovered one of the male houseguests in bed with a pantry boy.

Outraged, this femme formidable resigned on the spot.

Crisis! The fate of the nation hung upon mollifying this good woman. Sir Horace summoned a highranking Jesuit friend, who pondered the question and asked if he might have a word with the housekeeper, privately. This was promptly arranged, with the desired result. The housekeeper would resume her vital role forthwith.

Sir Horace was as intrigued as he was relieved. What stratagem had his Jesuit friend employed with such instant success? The prelate smiled. "I simply pointed out to your good lady that if she left now people would interpret her reaction as one of jealousy ..." Mat is always a welcome visitor to Heather Island, with his wry little anecdotes that leave one chuckling at every recollection.

February

R adio Telefís Éireann chirpily invited us to celebrate St. Brigid's Day, February 1st., the First Day of Spring. Morriagh! Even from the breakfast table in the kitchen (the warmest room in the house) I could see the waves crashing against the rocks on the shore. The weather forecast seemed more realistic: snow and ice, making driving conditions hazardous in all parts of the country. That was more like it, more in keeping with E. W. Nye's observation: "Winter lingered so long in the lap of Spring that it occasioned a great deal of talk." Anyway, who was St. Brigid, she of the curiously offset cross, made of woven rushes?

My father's 1924 (English) missal was somewhat dismissive, confining celebration of St. Brigid's Day to the dioceses of Birmingham and Portsmouth, though it did concede that Brigid had put Kildare on the map, becoming its first abbess. Brigid, a virgin, died on February 1st. 523 and was buried in Kildare. "Her body was afterwards translated to Downpatrick, in Ulster, where it lies beside that of St. Patrick and St. Columba." My 1960 (Glenstal Abbey) version proved much more fulsome, dignifying Brigid as the "Secondary Patroness of All Ireland and Principal Patroness of the diocese of Kildare and Leighlin". The Collect runs: "O God, you gladden us this day by the yearly festival of blessed Brigid your virgin; mercifully grant that we may be helped by the merits of her whose example of chastity shines upon us with such lustre: through our Lord." Six months' sojourn in Connemara made me wonder whether anyone advocating "chastity" would attract many followers down here, even though I had met a number of women called Brigid.

Having long since forgotten—if, indeed, I had ever learned—how to find my way through a Daily Missal, I became absorbed in looking through the Mass cards: Mary R. Williams, died 1944; Moira Williams, died 1946; Edmund Williams, died 1949; John Williams, died 1965. I remembered the last-named. He established a record haul of sea trout from the Dawros estuary, on the road to Letterfrack, that will stand for all time.

Then to my own Missal: Oliver St John Gogarty, died 1957, and also in there a holy picture: "To Guy in memory of his First Holy Communion, 9/6/55." My old governess, Miss Dix, Charleville Road, Tullamore, charged with teaching me the three Rs. The poor woman subsequently lost her reason and was committed to St. Patrick's, Dean Swift's memorial.

I recalled accompanying my mother down through the long, dingy, vaulted corridors, led by the nurse with her enormous, jangling key ring. I was petrified. Fears became tears at the pathetic sight of this once meticulous woman, reduced now to a gabbling old hag, scrambling to gather her few belongings and imploring my mother to take her away from that terrible place, then turning to me in frantic search of support ...

"Have you lost your hearing as well as your marbles? Alastair's on the 'phone!" "Hello, Guy, vermin competition. Rosleague, the shoreline. Saturday at dusk. Bring Nick if he's home. No dogs needed. OK. See you!" Letterfrack Gun Club traditionally scored well in these annual February—March competitions, which may say something about our gamekeeping efforts during the other ten months of the year. Nicholas was delighted to discover that his shooting season hadn't ended. This was much better fun than firing at boring old clays.

We took up our stations on the foreshore below the conifer plantation where the magpies and grey crows come in to roost at dusk—Gerry Carpets and his teenage son, Rory Daly, Gunter, Alastair, Nicholas and I—and waited for the evening flight to commence. Those further out opened fire first, deflecting their escapers down along the bay to our stands. Alastair seemed to score with every shot. Nicholas accounted for a respectable tally, while I brought something down with a splintering crash in the wood behind me. Then the search began for the cadavers, without which neither credit nor the bounty of fifty pence each would be forthcoming. Eventually, everything was picked up, except for my victim. As we trudged back up to Rosleague in the dark, Nicholas murmured to me that he was pretty sure that I had downed a heron. Naturally I assured him he was mistaken. What experienced sportsman could possibly confuse grey crows with herons?

It wasn't until a few nights later, when I went up to collect the stuffed snipe, that Alastair referred to the wounded heron that he had found and finished off ... "Strange, do you think it had been shot?" I asked. "Oh, no question about that. Its wing was shattered. Could have been one of the others further out along the point. Should know better."

"Dreadful carry-on. But tell me, Alastair, this fish farmers' conference in Clifden tomorrow, what's the score?" "Oh, that's always good for a laugh. Surprised you haven't been approached to join the protest march." I had, hence my quest for information. "It's the salmon farmers' annual show of strength. Malcolm and Geoffrey and Gerry Fish and Edwin Treacy are up to their tonsils organising it. I've got something up my sleeve for Geoffrey this time!"

The unwelcome "invitation" to join in this peaceful protest had come from two of the stalwarts of the Culfin Anglers' Club.

As residents of Lettergesh, they were incensed at the application by the fish farm in the mouth of the Killary for permission to put cages further out into the bay, where they would be visible from miles around, as well as posing a threat of pollution to pristine Glassilaun beach. The very situation that I so particularly wanted to avoid had arrived. It's at times like this that living on an island has its advantages. I could simply lie low that day. I did just that, spending the time staking out the area to be planted with the famous sycamores, due to arrive from Belgium any time soon.

At dusk I ventured down to Letterfrack, curious to hear of the day's events. Alastair was chortling into his pint, delighting in Geoffrey's evident discomfort. Around these parts everybody knows everybody else's car and cars are seldom locked, whatever about the drivers. So it had been all too easy for Alastair to insert a sign on the rear window ledge of Geoffrey's car, inciting all and sundry to: "SAVE OUR SEATROUT". The bewildered Geoffrey had found himself the butt of many jibes — not all of them in jest — before realising the cause. Now he was in search of the culprit.

Before Geoffrey got the opportunity to confirm his strong suspicions, the door swung open to admit the scarecrow figure of Stuart, tweed hat jammed down around his ears, jacket flapping as though the pockets contained ferrets fighting. Stuart was looking for a row: "So this is where you're skulking, you lousy fish farmers ..." But that was as far as Stuart got. With a speed and sense of purpose that did credit to his years, the landlord had seized this troublemaker and bundled him out into the night whence he had appeared, apologizing to anglers and fish farmers alike for Stuart's intrusion, adding that Stuart was presently persona non grata on this licensed premises. This landlord runs an orderly house, in which it is generally a pleasure to imbibe and socialise.

When the customary tenor of conversation returned,

Batman and Gerry Park recalled the occasion on which a veritable giant of a man, crazed with drink, had burst into the pub, roaring abuse and threatening to take the place and all within it apart. The mild-mannered landlord had vaulted his counter, grabbed the giant in a headlock, hustled him out the door and locked it before anyone had time to react. This display of courage and competence had added enormously to the landlord's reputation, in a society where violence lurks ever so close to the surface.

Not that violence had ever touched the life of Sister Brendan OSB, the first member of the Kylemore Community to end her days beyond the confines of the convent. Sister Brendan was a member of the Walsh family from Mullaghgloss—and not from Lettergesh, as she was wont to emphasise—the family that Mitchell Henry had imported from faraway Tipperary as ploughmen, that skill being unknown in the vicinity then; as it is forgotten now. She must have been one of the first pupils in Kylemore school, which opened in 1921, for she had gone there at the age of fourteen, been professed in 1927 and had only ever left the precincts to go into hospital in Galway. So strict were the rules under which Sister Brendan had taken her vows, she was forbidden to visit her sister, who lived literally at the gates of Kylemore, just as she was obliged to watch her mother's funeral cortege from the windows of the castle as it passed over the causeway between the Kylemore lakes. Her successors fly around the world, fundraising.

The initial advertisement in *The Irish Times* of 30 July 1921 makes interesting reading all these years on. "The first Monastic School for girls to flourish in Ireland since the sixteenth century is now being opened at Kylemore Abbey. It is conducted by the Irish Benedictine Nuns, who have preserved all their ancient traditions of giving their pupils a thoroughly sound and complete training, according to the fundamental tenets laid down by Saint Benedict in his Monastic Rule.

"In accordance with the long-standing traditions of monastic education, moral development receives primary and careful attention. The family spirit, tempered with an atmosphere of refinement and culture, the distinctive mark of the Benedictine system, pervades the school life of the pupils. The girls are admitted at an early age, and all branches of their education and instruction are undertaken or supervised by the Nuns.

"The School curriculum includes the Christian Doctrine, the Irish Language, History and Literature, English Language do., Classical and Modern European Languages, Geography, Modern History, Science and Mathematics. Junior Pupils are taught on modern methods, while the senior girls receive instruction in Home Science and the Fine Arts. There are special facilities for good Musical Training, Voice Culture and French and German conversation. All pupils follow courses in Dancing and Physical Culture, and must take part in the Games.

"The Abbey is ideally adapted for scholastic purposes. It occupies one of the most unique positions in Europe, amidst the savage grandeur of the Connemara Highlands, unrivalled for their scenic beauty of mountain, ocean, lake and river. The pupils enjoy the benefit of organised rambles and excursions."

Fundraising was a feature of monastic existence then as now, as the legendary Dick Duggan, one of the founders of the Irish Hospitals Sweepstakes, discovered to his cost. The newly established *Irish Press* related the story in November 1931. "When Mr. Duggan ran a sweep in connection with Kylemore Abbey Convent, then the home of a number of exiled Belgian nuns, he ran foul of what was then the law.

"These nuns were in dire straits, and they asked Mr. Duggan to give them his aid. At this period the Government were 'down' on sweeps, and Mr. Duggan, caught napping on a technicality, found himself charged with being a 'rogue and a vagabond'. Not a ticket for the Kylemore sweep was sold in

Ireland, but the tickets had been printed in Ireland. This was a breach of the law — a minute one may be, but nevertheless an offence — and Mr. Duggan was put under arrest, and brought before the Bench as 'a rogue and a vagabond' — the technical — and absurd — phrase used by the law for an offender under the Act.

"The sentence was three months, but it had not to be served as the First Offenders' Act was successfully brought into play."

The image of the cowled and wimpled nuns, facing penury in their vast Gothic castle, "amidst the savage grandeur of the Connemara Highlands", causing a co-founder of the Irish Hospitals' Sweepstakes organisation to face a term in gaol is rich indeed. It would surely have found a place in the amazing, fantastical memoirs of George O'Malley, from nearby Keelkyle. Following in his father's footsteps, George had become a renowned smuggler of tobacco and wines from the Channel Islands into Ballynakill Bay. In retirement he wrote his reminiscences, which have remained unpublished to date, as nobody has been able to sort out what material is original and what is plagiarism. This seems a shame, for indigenous literature is scarce in Connemara.

February had almost run its course when the first signs of Spring manifested themselves, in the form of tractorloads of seaweed, collected from the highwater mark, being spread on the fields surrounding Tully Lake. Our appreciation of this admirable exercise in organic manuring was soon qualified, for the odour of the decomposing seaweed suggested not so much manure as human ordure. More shades of Macau, where ordure is highly esteemed in vegetable cultivation. Tommy Joyce, on whose fields our ESB poles now stood in unsightly profusion, began his methodical spreading of farmyard manure, accumulated over the winter, when his cattle were housed each night. Martin Golden's field was all of a sudden covered in ewes, coming close to lambing, which happens late in the season down here.

John B. Keane's play, *The Field*, finds echoes in the way in which Martin Golden tends the long, long pasture that slopes down to the lakeshore. Whatever the time of year, Martin can be seen cleaning drains, spreading manure, topping thistles, mending fences, dosing sheep, herding cattle or rounding up his prize-winning Connemara mare and foal to take them to a local show. Immensely proud of his Connemara ponies, Martin becomes uncharacteristically voluble on the rare occasions that they fail to take first prize, bewailing the incompetence of modern-day judges. He may have a point. After a lifetime's "following" Connemaras, Martin has forgotten more about the breed than most will ever learn. His famous stallion, Kimble, has long since become part of local legend.

Often, on the worst of winter days, Martin can be seen, silently observing our crabwise progress through the waves. By the time we have made the safety of the shore he has disappeared about his solitary business, for Martin Golden is not one to "put talk on you", as Stan the Shovel is wont to describe conversational overtures. Having delegated his business concerns to his sons, Bill and Ron, Martin devotes his days to the land, with an intensity that can sometimes feel intimidating. For a quick-tempered man, this self-imposed solitude seems sensible.

Golden's shop, post office and pub form a nucleus in Tully village, where Edmond Golden is recorded in Griffith's Valuation of 1855 as being liable for £3-10-0 rates on his house, office and garden. These covered an area of 10 perches (300 square yards). Edmond's landlord, Henry Blake of Renvyle, owned and farmed 4,900 acres—the entire peninsula, in addition to the 8,194 acres let to Canon Wilberforce and another 824 acres leased to Hamilton C. Smith, Clerk of the Clifden Board of Guardians.

If Winter continued to sit in the lap of Spring, as it did, it was mild in comparison to the weather on the continent, which continued to delay the despatch of those eagerly awaited sycamores. It wasn't so much that I relished the prospect of digging over two thousand holes, inserting a similar number of sycamore "whips" and footing them in firmly. I didn't. The urgency lay in getting them planted before they should begin to leaf, and before the undergrowth should begin to flourish again. Mr. Foyle had been emphatic on this point, predicting dire failure rates from delayed planting.

Milady's resumption in Kylemore Abbey, where she was put in charge of booking in coach tours for the season ahead, prompted the idea of setting up literary tours of Connemara. Discussions with Michael Gibbons led me to Kevin Joyce, historian, bibliophile and proprietor of an elegant craft shop in Recess. Like Michael, Kevin is infectiously enthusiastic on anything likely to promote the "hidden" aspects of Connemara. We planned our itinerary on a day-long tour from Galway.

The first port of call must be Ross House, home of Violet Martin, the "Ross" of Somerville & Ross, whose *Through Connemara in a Governess Cart*, written in 1893, would dictate our route. Moycullen we discounted, for virtually nothing remains of Danesfield, the ancestral home of the Burkes, or de Burgos as they had styled themselves when coming to Ireland with Strongbow. Daisy Burke had married Lord Fingall in 1883, at the age of seventeen, going on to become one of the most influential figures in Anglo-Irish society. While her husband pursued his passion for foxhunting, Daisy Fingall devoted her considerable energy to assisting her husband's cousin, Sir Horace Plunkett, in his lifelong crusade to establish agricultural co-operatives throughout Ireland, thus freeing the farmers from the grip of the middlemen. Fingall died in 1929; Plunkett three years later. In 1937 Daisy Fingall published her memoirs, *Seventy Years Young*, an extraordinarily vivid and enthralling account of "Castle" society in Ireland and a caste that had virtually disappeared in the aftermath of the Treaty of 1922. The original manuscript was rumoured to contain racy passages, omitted when caution prevailed. *Seventy Years Young* becomes more tantalising for these omissions, leaving the reader to make as he will of such throwaway remarks as: "My dear man, I never slept with either King Edward or Sir Horace Plunkett!" Republished in 1991 by Lilliput Press, Daisy Fingall's autobiography has been in print ever since; deservedly so.

Ross House—our first stop—lay derelict until being purchased and lavishly restored by George and Elizabeth McLaughlin from New York. George is a natural raconteur, delighting in regaling his listeners with the history of the house and its eccentric inhabitants down through the ages since Robert Martin came into possession in 1590. One of the latest in that long line, a Chavasse, sported an enormous red beard, wore a kilt and refused to converse other than in Gaelic. Saved from certain death through the cries of a chambermaid, who had spotted the roof timbers burning, Chavasse had rebuilt his ruin using no timber, only steel and concrete. Fortunately, the present incumbents do not share that paranoia. The interior is as exquisite as the exterior is imposing. Morning coffee will be taken in Ross House.

Oughterard, the fishing village at the foot of Loch Corrib, is flanked by literary landmarks. The graveyard where James Joyce pictured the resting place of Michael Furey in "The Dead"—"the snow falling faintly ... faintly falling"—lies at the eastern approach. Beyond it is Lemonfield, the sadly reduced home of the o'fflaherties, legendary rulers of Connemara. Ruined before World War II, Lemonfield had contained the Letters patent granted by Elizabeth I to Sir Morrough na dtuagh (of the Battle-axe) o'fflahertie, granted in return for his oath of fealty to her, encompassing his territory of Connemara, his castles and his fleet on Loch Corrib.

At the western end of Oughterard is Clare Villa, once upon a time styled as "Dick Martin's gate lodge", and subsequently the home of George Bernard Shaw's mother; an association that Shaw seems actively to have disparaged. But then Shaw's relations with the land of his birth were always ambivalent. Did he not comment to Lady Gregory on the fact that three of the most "indecent" writers in the English language were Irish—Frank Harris, George Moore and James Joyce?

On entering into Connemara proper we would make reference to the Galway—Clifden railway line, with its 700-foot cutting near the village. It was to this site that historical novelist Walter Macken was repeatedly drawn, feeling that it represented the most graphic symbol of the hope that the completion of the railway in 1895 offered to the denizens of this wild and desolate land.

At Maam Cross, that ancient crossing point of drovers' trails and site of markets and fairs from time immemorial, we must decide whether to make a detour to our left, to Screeb and thence to Rosmuc, where Patrick Pearse built his simple summer cottage and dreamed of "an Ireland free". Among Pearse's visitors to his cottage in Rosmuc was said to have been Count Lev Nikolaevich Tolstoi. He travelled by train to Maam Cross, completing his journey by sidecar to Rosmuc. The alternative is to keep straight on to Recess.

However, before making any such decision, we must allude to a Victorian writer born in the vicinity. Totally forgotten today, William Francis Lynam (*c.* 1845–1894) commanded an enormous following with his serialised adventures of "Mick M'Quaid, cottier, cock-fighter, Ribbonman, labourer and guide to the Western Highlands", many of them originating on the shores of Lough Shindilla, to the west of Maam Cross. Among Lynam's quaintly-titled novels were *Souperina Noodle*, *Japhet Screw* and *Corney Cluskey's Calamities*. Besides being good yarns, Lynam's writings were thinly disguised diatribes against the

Established Church and the despised campaigns of "souperism".

Growing thirsty from all this talk of things literary, we resolved to forsake the starkness of Rosmuc and its "Teach an Phiarsaigh" for the welcome shelter of Paddy Festy's in Recess. Kevin Joyce's emporium dominates this tiny hamlet, which derives its English name from a farmstead named "The Recess", which was leased from the Martins of Ballynahinch by one William Andrews in 1846. Kevin likes to give his late father the credit for literally putting Recess on the map. This he did by securing the local agency for "Caltex" petrol when motoring was a novelty in Ireland. As part of their promotional efforts the petrol companies published huge quantities of motoring maps, none more assiduously than the California-Texas Oil Co. The original petrol pump installed outside Joyce's in Recess has been carefully preserved in tribute to that entrepreneur.

From Recess we set forth to Ballynahinch Castle, now a gracious and most comfortable country hotel, offering the finest of salmon fishing within a stone's throw of the Martins' former stronghold. Somerville & Ross were preceded here by William Thackeray as he compiled his *Irish Sketch Book* and also by Maria Edgeworth. In the panelled bar, under the doleful gaze of a contemporary impression of Granuaile, the Pirate Queen of the Western Ocean, we deliberated on a programme of readings and recitals to regale our literary tourists over their lunch.

Clifden—the capital of Connemara—posed a challenge, for we could not come up with any literary associations whatsoever. True, we thought of Kate O'Brien in Roundstone and Alannah Heather in Errislannan and, indeed, of the poet Richard Murphy's wellknown association with Cleggan, to the northwest. But Clifden itself? Nothing ... Our next stop would have to be Ballynakill cemetery, resting place of Oliver St.

John Gogarty and his wife, Martha. Ulick O'Connor's account
of the symbolic flight from Cartron Lake of that solitary swan
as Gogarty's coffin was being lowered into the grave would be
particularly apt at this juncture; Gogarty being fascinated
throughout his life by these fabled creatures.

> "Keep you these calm and lovely things,
> And float them on your clearest water;
> For one would not disgrace a King's
> Transformed beloved and buoyant daughter.
>
> "And with her goes this sprightly swan,
> A bird of more than royal feather,
> With alban beauty clothed upon;
> O keep them fair and well together!"

We should not quit Ballynakill without reference to
Gogarty's good friend, Dermot Freyer, for his son, Michael
Freyer lives close by. Dermot Freyer, whose father, Sir Peter,
also a Connemara man, had been the first to perfect the
prostate gland operation, was one of a distinguished quartet—
George Moore, Augustus John and Séamus O'Sullivan were
the others—to receive copies of Gogarty's first volume of
poetry, *Hyperthuleana* (Beyond the Beyonds). Of the five copies
printed in 1916, Gogarty kept the remaining one himself.
Dermot Freyer was an accomplished poet and author in his
own right; *Not All Joy* being a collection of his short stories that
are timeless, convey a lovely quality of imagination and reveal
glimpses of a delightful character. It is a volume that, once
procured, should never, never be loaned, not to no one!

Like Gogarty, Dermot Freyer became an hotelier, in the
remotest reaches of Achill Island, where the modus operandi
was sufficiently bizarre to move young Dermot Gogarty to
write:

"Many things are very queer
In the house of Dermot Freyer!"

One of my own early recollections of the west concerned an expedition with my parents to Achill to visit the good Major, as he was known. Drinks were dispensed from a cupboard under the staircase and payment was inserted into an RNLI collection box, a liquor licence forming no part of the attributes of the Major's hostelry.

Such symbiotic association as this should pave the way for our visit to Renvyle House, thus resuming in the footsteps of Somerville & Ross. Here a veritable cornucopia of literary enlightenment could encompass the spectrum from John Mahaffy, Yeats and Rosetti to Ian Fleming. The last-named was only accredited to Renvyle House after lengthy deliberation, for he belongs more precisely to Heather Island, one of his western seaboard trysting spots.

The problem, we conceded, with Heather Island becoming part of our proposed itinerary, concerned its accessibility, which was totally dependent upon clement weather in which to ferry our literary-minded tourists back and forth, not to mention the time involved in such an exercise. It seemed a better bet to "donate" James Bond's creator to Renvyle and concentrate instead on another island, which is accessible by means of a short causeway—Illaun Rua, or Lady Wilde's Island. This would be the first landmark on the return journey to Galway.

Lady Wilde's Island, close by the shores of Lough Fee, was built by Oscar's parents as a summer house in the west, where the youthful Oscar sported and played with his brother Willie. Both Oscar's father and mother were prolific writers in the cause of Irish nationalism, his mother adopting the nom de plume "Speranza". Sir William Wilde's *Loch Corrib* remains the seminal work of reference on that inland sea. The split-level lodge contains a mural—"Light Lines"—painted by Oscar's artist friend, George Francis Miles, while on holiday there.

This effectively completed our odyssey around the literary landmarks of Connemara. The rest of the return journey would thus be available for discussion of the day's experiences. This, we agreed, could be the most fraught element of the whole undertaking, the point at which our accounts of people and places could come under an uncomfortable degree of scrutiny, quite possibly by those whose knowledge considerably outweighed our own ... Kevin felt sure that many of our prospective sightseers would contribute quite a lot of additional information. That would be welcome indeed, as long as it didn't conflict diametrically with our own version, on matters of fact. Opinions wouldn't matter, very much.

It was with a light heart that I approached Áras Fáilte, off Eyre Square, and an appointment with one of the prime movers in Ireland West Tourism. Kevin had pleaded a prior engagement. If politics is the art of the possible, then Connemara tourism must be the pursuit of the impossible. For such was the reception accorded to our "brainchild". There are important differences between devil's advocacy and negative thinking. I encountered the latter and departed disillusioned. Kevin was philosophical, pointing out that "Galway" means "town of the stranger" in Irish and rightly so, for its inhabitants regard every fiver that crosses westwards over the salmon weir bridge as a fiver lost to the greedy burghers of that town.

By way of distraction, Kevin drew my attention to an item in the paper proposing the restoration of the Galway—Clifden railway line, closed some sixty years ago, after only forty years in existence. The anonymous contributor estimated that a mere twelve million pounds would restore the permanent way, with a similar amount required to replace the bridges and the halts at Moycullen, Oughterard, Maam, Recess and Ballynahinch: "the idea seems an excellent one and perhaps should be studied by the proliferating quango-like groups now bent on saving the west." Had I ever considered writing a book on the old railway, from its completion in 1895 to its demise in 1935?

I had indeed. But first I wanted to walk its forty-eight miles. But not in February. No, definitely not in February, nor March, nor even April. That was a high summer project. Though hardly of the train-spotting persuasion, I had always been fascinated by that Galway–Clifden railway line, having been brought up on stories of my mother boarding the night sleeper at Euston station and having lunch in Clifden the following day. We haven't improved very much on that record, all these years later. Another appeal of the Galway–Clifden line — or what remains of it — to me is the fact that it is virtually the only permanent mark made by Man on the Connemara landscape; the cuttings, the embankments, the cut stone bridges all remain as silent witness to this monumental human lifeline that finally brought the western reaches of outermost Connemara into regular contact with the rest of Ireland and thence the wider world beyond. The legend of the rails from the Clifden end being lifted, sold and freighted out of Clifden on a German ship, subsequently to be recast as bomb casings and dropped on London during the Blitz only added more colour to this most romantic of bygone railway lines.

Ireland West Tourism's negative reaction to our concept of literary tours of Connemara may have had its origins in recent Bord Fáilte research overseas. This had revealed that foreigners perceived Ireland as being green and wet and engrossed in the consumption of black beer; no place to bring women and children on holidays. This we learned at a symposium in Galway, designed to convey Bord Fáilte's ambitious plans for Irish tourism in the new millennium. The response to this remarkable exposition was restrained, for most of the attendance seemed more immediately concerned with the present than the distant future. I shared this concern, anxious to ascertain what level of support I might receive in opening Heather Island to the public as a place of historic interest. That was a quite different kettle of fish.

March

***

The daffodils that have shot up so bravely all over those parts of the island that afford any shelter at all seem able to withstand everything that this mad month of March can hurl at them, as they shake their yellow heads in confusion. Against the burly Plover they have no defence. The two dogs—joined occasionally by the anonymous cat—delight in tearing around the lawn, burning off surplus energy. Plover's particular pleasure is in finding herself upended in a clump of daffodils. Her other boisterous ploy is cannoning into the backs of our knees in her headlong charge to the pier, ecstatic at the prospect of a raid on the village and its canine population. Teal, in contrast, flits, shadow-like, ever on the alert for game that may have opted to lie low. She misses little in that respect.

"The girls"—as they have been dubbed—have evolved their own routines for these lake crossings. Plover plants her front paws squarely on the thwart facing the rower for most of the crossing, apparently unmindful of Teal's stealthy sortie beneath the thwarts up to the bows, in readiness for docking on the mainland. Plover waits until the rower stows the pier-side oar. This is her signal to lunge to the bows, shoving Teal aside and leaping on to the pier, defying her companion to follow suit. Life is a lark, to Plover. Teal, disdaining further hurly-burly when there may be game lying in store, skips nimbly out on the other side and sets off in search of her quarry. Teal is a gundog, which Plover—so far anyway—shows no sign of becoming.

In one respect we seem to have succeeded in educating this ill-assorted duo. They can resist any temptation to chase sheep, however provoking those silly creatures may be. Scattering in all directions at the first hint of a potential pursuer, they invite pursuit. Martin Golden's ewes are all heavily in lamb at this time. His flock are not kept alive solely to qualify for subsidies and thus avoid the Irish Wildlife Federation's spokesman's epithet, "woolly locusts".

Tom O'Byrne of the IWF rattled a few cages when he denounced the depredations caused by overgrazing of the mountains, particularly in winter, pointing out that the sparse vegetation was being cut away by the hooves of these starving "woolly locusts". The loosened soil was being washed away, leaving only bare rock. Wildlife film maker Éamon de Buitléar had added his voice, declaring that the blanket bog covering the hillsides was slipping down into the rivers and lakes below, leaving desolation that it could take a thousand years to repair. The Department of Agriculture conceded by way of response that sheep numbers in the State, estimated at 8.67 million, were somewhat higher than was generally considered desirable.

Such agronomic exchanges were far from the mind of one Kurt Kaiser, as he attempted to find guest speakers in the locality to enlighten and entertain his students of Anglo-Irish literature, encamped for their winter semester in the Connemara West thatched cottages that form one side of Tullycross village. "Would Mr. Williams be so kind as to address the class on Oliver St John Gogarty, his grandfather?"

"Why, of course. He'd love to!", said Milady, in her instantly assumed role of literary agent and promoter.

The massed students of Aquinas College, Michigan, crowded into the livingroom of one cottage, proved difficult to enthuse. They appeared satiated with literature, learning and erudition. In the end I resorted to regaling them with stories of the Renvyle House ghost. This was more like it, humanising W. B. Yeats, in his unaccustomed role as transcriber of his wife's seance, at which the ghost of poor little Ethelred Henry Blake was summoned to appear. The encounter took place in the room in which the unfortunate boy had been incarcerated, having been certified insane. Through his wife's psychic powers, Yeats issued five demands to this troubled soul; essentially to cease and desist from menacing the Gogarty family in their recently acquired country house. The apparition conveyed to Mrs. Yeats that he resented strangers in the house of his ancestors and then agreed that he could be placated by incense and flowers. They loved the yarn, so far removed from scansion and iambic pentameters.

Over a pint in the Anglers' Rest, Kurt conceded that his students could have been suffering from an "overload" of Anglo-Irish literature, and thus more amenable to an evening of legend instead. As for the contrast between Michigan and Tullycross ... he had been born and raised in a village in Minnesota, founded by German settlers.

Like Tullycross, his village was dominated by a towering church. He found many other similarities between his isolated village in Minnesota and the remoteness of Connemara communities. As for his students ... they would get almost as many credits for attendance on this voyage of exploration as they would for their academic accomplishments. It was an interesting extension of the concept of "cultural exchange". It was, in many ways, a course in anthropology.

The west of Ireland has attracted anthropologists from America from the time that Americans first discovered this interest in the study of other cultures. The Greeks had been recording their observations since the time of Xenophanes and Herodotus, some five hundred years BC. Of more recent vintage was a Norwegian with the unlikely name of Colm

Murphy. He had invited himself to stay for a weekend with Tom Joyce in Shanakeever—and there remained for six months, until removed by his brother from Oslo.

Kraken has been around these parts considerably longer, seventeen years in fact, during which he has added much local lore to an already considerable general knowledge. The combined intellects of Alastair the chef, Batman the ranger, Kraken and the writer, finding themselves in convivial proximity along the Trading Post's bar counter, cheerfully consented to enter as a team in the pub quiz being broadcast over the airwaves from Connemara FM, just across the road. Teams have entered from pubs throughout Connemara. An invigilator in each hostelry is charged with handing out the blank answer forms, collecting the completed forms at each stage and telephoning each team's scores to the radio station. We are extremely bullish about success, for no other intellectual quartet can possibly boast such an awesome arsenal of useless knowledge.

Through some inexplicable combination of circumstances, our answers, though correct in every instance—we had no doubt of that—signally failed to correspond to those sought by quizzmistress, Mary Roe. Not only were we not adjudged the winners, we didn't feature in the first ten! With the incalculable benefit of hindsight it occurred to us that we may have over-trained for the event, having commenced imbibing some hours before Round One. Nor was our downfall confined to matters intellectual ... Kraken toppled off his bar stool when attempting to adjust his shoelaces. Such an occurrence might well have been forgotten, had Lewis's lady wife not happened to overhear a remark in a restaurant in Galway the very next day. Two people, observing a high chair being produced for an infant, agreed that such could come in handy in the Trading Post.

Mary Roe's disembodied voice over the airwaves brought

back childhood memories of Mary's grandmother, who had lived in the lee of Letter Hill, that "great rock" sheltering Heather Island from the prevailing winds. Mrs. Little had been the cook on Heather Island forty years ago and more. A boat had been kept on the south side of the island to ferry Mrs. Little to and fro. The back kitchen—disused for many years now—had boasted a turf stove and a paraffin cooker. When both of those were at full blast it was quite impossible to see into the kitchen for smoke and equally difficult to breathe for paraffin fumes. Yet, without fail, at or near the appointed hour, Mrs. Little would emerge from this hell-hole, flushed but triumphant, to hammer the gong that stood in the serving hatch. Her stentorian cries; "Yer dinner's ready!" made the gong superfluous, mere ritual really.

Ritual had formed a very great part of my grandmother Gogarty's eccentric existence. Lunch was always "luncheon" and the ladies withdrew to the "withdrawingroom". Mrs. Gogarty conducted her correspondence from her escritoire in her "morningroom", just off the diningroom. Even her husband became exasperated with his wife's airs and graces from time to time. On one occasion, when asked how his wife was keeping, Gogarty replied: "She's grand, and getting grander. Thank you."

Though I grew up in fear of this haughty old dame swathed in black and furs, those who recall her around these parts invariably do so with affection, citing the extraordinary devotion she commanded from her menagerie of animals that followed her everywhere she went on foot. These included sundry dogs and cats, a sheep, a goat and even a gander. The last-named made casual conversation impossible. In its self-appointed role as its mistress's protector and bodyguard, it would rush, neck outstretched, hissing at anyone and everyone, irrespective of their intentions.

As became a lady of her standing, my grandmother never

learned to drive, employing instead a succession of chauffeurs to fulfil this function in a series of huge black saloons. During the rebuilding of Renvyle House she would walk the four miles from O'Grady's Hotel in Letterfrack to oversee progress, returning by the same means, accompanied on her way by that extraordinary assembly of animals, and the ferocious gander. To attempt such a manoeuvre today would be foolhardy, but in those days motor cars were a rarity on the roads around here. Even in the 'fifties cars were scarce, and the arrival of the CIE bus or delivery lorry a social occasion.

Tom Joyce paints a heartrending picture of emigration throughout the 'fifties and 'sixties, when each teenager was duly confronted with the daunting prospect: "O God, my turn next." The taxi would be hired, taking the emigrant, parents and assorted siblings to Shannon and what was all-too-often a final farewell. The street names of Boston, London and New York were familiar to all growing up in Connemara, whereas of Dublin nothing was known, for there was no opportunity there for Connemara youth. For the sons that stayed behind there were no girls to marry when that time came. He could recall a dance at Maam — 172 males, 40 females and a fight to gain the favour of a spinster long past her prime.

It was to draw wider attention to this haemorrhage of the west that John Healy wrote his famous plea, *No one cried Stop*, Fr. McDyer set up Glencolumcille and, a few years later, Connemara West was born. From its incorporation in 1971, funded by community investment averaging £20 per household, Connemara West progressed through the Rent an Irish Cottage scheme in Tullycross, through the creation of the Teach Ceoil in Tully to the purchase and renovation of the abandoned Industrial School in Letterfrack. What started off as a woodworking course in 1982 is today a fully accredited University degree course, while the experiment with North Connemara Community Radio in 1988 has blossomed into

Connemara FM, an often-spirited forum for lively debate on issues of concern to the widespread, scattered populace it serves.

One has only to look across the road from the Trading Post and see the fleet of cars parked outside what was for years a forbidding, dilapidated and deserted building to begin to appreciate the transformation that Connemara West has wrought upon the whole community. The influx of woodworking students has been a breath of fresh air in a traditionally tightly knit society, besides bringing welcome off-season revenue.

The neatly pollarded chestnut trees that flank the road in front of the Connemara West headquarters herald the coming of summer each year and symbolise, somehow, the security and prosperity that was James Ellis's vision when he transformed Letterfrack a hundred and fifty years ago.

Prior to the coming of James Ellis, the Blakes had described Letterfrack in their *Letters from the Irish Highlands*: "In every rood of ground you trace the absence of a fostering hand; while the miserable cabins, falling in ruins around you, repeat the same melancholy tale. The rattle of carriage wheels was a sound quite new to the wild natives, and they peeped out of their lowly dwellings with an aspect scarcely human; their long dark hair, tangled over their neck and shoulders, and their bright black eyes but just discernible through the half-opened door." And that description was penned more than twenty years before the Famine.

This preoccupation with the history of north Connemara may seem irrelevant to some, but it happens to be a constantly recurring aspect of everyday existence down here. Only this month the laying of a new road further into the turf bogs of windswept Crocnaraw led to the discovery of a Bronze Age burial site, indicated by two toppled white quartz standing stones, symbols of innocence, power or death. In this instance they would seem to have signified both innocence and death, for scientific analysis of the human ashes found in a pottery urn underneath the stones revealed them to be of a twelve-year-old, dating from some 1500 years BC.

When Michael Gibbons spoke to the media of this find as further evidence of the pre-historic "sacred hills" of Connemara and the population explosion in the area between 3,000 and 4,000 years ago, with more and more coming to light as each day passes, he conjured up visions of a landscape as different from today's as it within the power of one's imagination to visualise. The site in Crocnaraw might be in the steppes of Russia, for there is no sign of human existence within three hundred and sixty degrees, unless you allow the clamps of turf and the vapour trails of jets streaming overhead.

This continual overlapping of the ancient and the contemporary was further emphasised by the furious reaction throughout Mayo and north Connemara to the issue of mining licences being granted in seventy townlands between Westport and the Killary. In an impassioned letter to *The Irish Times*, Paddy Hopkins, Chairman of the Mayo Environmental Group, asserted: "the campaign will be launched against those who are the real threat to our environment and our growing tourist industry, the politicians. The intelligent, wideawake people here will not stand idly by ... We have the good fortune to live in a lovely place, conscious of our clean environment ... No government or minister will ever be allowed to hand it over to the destructive processes of mining."

Paddy's late father, "Peter the Pilot", would have been proud of his son's spirited defence of the environment in which he had spent his life piloting ships in and out of Westport harbour, through the 365 islands that dot Clew Bay. "Hoppy", as Peter was also known, had already retired when I first met him as a small boy. Lean and tanned, with clear blue eyes and a white moustache, Peter Hopkins kept and crewed my father's

pucaun, sailing from the pier below his house on the road to
Murrisk. It was Peter who fostered my love for the sea and
taught me all I know about seafishing. He was also a fund of
stories about the sea, claiming to have seen the Flying
Dutchman on more than one occasion.

Having lit his pipe and settled himself at the tiller, Peter
Hopkins would quietly advise my father, Peter Luke, Louis le
Brocquy and anyone else on board where best to look for
mackerel, pollock, skate and tope. He could call on a lifetime's
knowledge of Clew Bay, its tides, winds and most likely
catching grounds, while always keeping a look out for any
signs of deteriorating weather conditions. Clew Bay is
deceptive in terms of its sheer size and Peter made a point of
never venturing too far from the lee of the islands, knowing the
limitations of the venerable Perkins "Handy Billy".

One day Peter, my father and I went after skate, heaving to
over a particularly favoured skate hole. The heavy cane sea rod
was set up, the hook baited with a lump of freshly caught
mackerel and carried to the sea bed by a lead weight. Within
moments it seemed that we had fouled either the hook or the
weight, for the line simply would not retract. Suddenly the reel
screeched as the line flew out almost to the full extent of the
backing line. We were into something monstrous! And so it
proved. After three hours fighting this unseen monster of the
deep we eventually brought a massive skate to the surface, by
which time we were too exhausted to gaff the brute and hoist
him aboard. Peter and my father sought to revive themselves
with tumblers of Tullamore Dew, while I stood ineffectually on
guard over the equally exhausted skate. By the time we
chugged back into Westport and had our prize hoisted and
weighed with block and tackle he tipped the scales at 96 lbs. —
just a few pounds short of an Irish specimen.

Those were the halcyon days of the pucaun, cherished as she
was by a seafarer who took pride in his craft. When the years

eventually caught up with "Hoppy" and he asked to be relieved of his responsibilities, we moved the boat down to Letterfrack pier, where Eddie and Liz O'Brien of Rosleague kept their boats. A sudden storm caught her on the weather side of the pier. She sprang a plank and foundered. For many years afterwards her burnt remains could be seen on the shore below Rosleague. Time and tide have now removed even these. The "lucky" eyes painted by Louis le Brocquy were salvaged from their places on the bows of the pucaun and are now above the hall door of Heather Island; keepsake and memento.

Yarns of yesteryear meant something altogether different to grand vizier, aesthete and merchant prince John Coyle, proprietor of Renvyle House. I was summoned to his weekly breakfast board meetings in the hotel to report progress on *A Sea-grey House*. The text was by now virtually complete and most of the illustrations to hand. It was time to engage a designer. John tracked down that gifted poster painter, Jan Voske, an exile from East Germany, who had stayed in Galway "a day too many", some years ago and was now living in a mobile home in Kinvara. His posters for the Galway and Clifden Arts Festivals had long since become collectors' items.

Jan was duly captured and whisked out to Renvyle in the executive Daimler. He seemed somewhat bewildered at finding himself involuntarily back in the setting of mercifully forgotten rampaging. The sensuous depiction of "The Wedding of Dionysus and Ariadne", that confronted him in the hotel diningroom, appeared to unnerve him completely, as he wandered the precincts in morose pursuit of features to record with a borrowed camera.

Jan's gloom deepened to despair on being informed by his patron that the "naked ladies", so prominent in Mary Waters' depiction of the wedding feast, should feature prominently on the dustjacket of *A Sea-grey House*. With his black felt hat and his straggling black beard, Jan looked like a latterday

Augustus John, who had stayed and painted in Renvyle House many years before. Augustus hadn't always seen eye to eye with his patron in Renvyle either.

The story goes that Mrs. Gogarty agreed to sit for Augustus; the portrait to be offset against his ever-escalating bar bill. When the painting was eventually completed Augustus mounted it on two high-backed chairs in the library for the ceremonial unveiling. Dr. Gogarty was invited to attend, naturally enough, for the painter and the surgeon-poet had long been friends and drinking companions. In front of the assembled guests Augustus unveiled the portrait with a flourish. Gogarty, scandalised, declared that such a likeness of his wife could never have been captured within the constraints of a professional relationship between painter and sitter. Screaming with rage, the volatile artist ran headlong at the canvas and jumped clean through it! One photograph exists as evidence of the portrait, that otherwise never was, or not for long.

Jan Voske returned to Galway in the back of John Coyle's plush Daimler, racking his brain for ways to resolve the conflict between his employer's wishes and his own artistic integrity. He confided his dilemma to one Andy Dolan, proprietor of the renowned Winkle's Hotel in Kinvara and the driving force behind the Fleadh na gCuach (Cuckoo Festival) to be held in Kinvara at the end of April. Strong on musical acts, but light on the literary side, Andy Dolan got in touch to enquire the possibility of putting on a Gogarty play in Dunguaire Castle on the outskirts of the seaside village.

Blight: The Tragedy of Dublin had played to full houses in the old Abbey theatre as long ago as 1917, as had *The Enchanted Trousers* two years later. At the time Gogarty had refused to admit authorship, for fear of consequences for his family and his medical practice. Both plays aroused much controversy at that time, dealing, as they do, with social hypocrisy. Seán

O'Casey, in his autobiography, revealed that "Blight" was one of the few Abbey plays he had seen before beginning his dramatic career and the similarities between "Blight" and *Juno and the Paycock* are readily apparent.

Gratifying though Andy's invitation was, the sheer time constraints made it impossible to accept. Not one to give up easily, Andy found two Galway thespians prepared to script and stage their own dramatised version of *As I Was Going Down Sackville Street*—an intriguing concept. The faithful of the Gogarty Society were notified of this unexpected happening. The venue could hardly be more appropriate, for Gogarty had bought the ruined 16th century castle during his castle-collecting phase, putting a studded door on it to keep out straying cattle and sheep.

All this literary business threatened to obliterate those seasonal opportunities to regenerate the grounds of Heather Island, where the first, cautious signs of spring were beginning to appear. The orchard, transplanted from its original site to the tennis court by the Duke of Leinster during the war, had fallen into a parlous state, through the depredations of goats and rams and years of neglect. The twins' half-term seemed an appropriate time to commence our assault.

Our first task was to cut back and uproot the sallies and rhododendrons that had encroached on three sides. On the remaining, southern side the once-neat laurel hedge had grown into trees twenty feet high. If they were also cut back to the butt they might, in time, regrow as a hedge, of sorts. Alastair came over with his cherished chainsaw and we set to work. At the end of that day's felling and sawing into logs for firewood I was absolutely knackered, whereas Alastair appeared to be still quite fresh. Dismayed at this contrast, for I had assumed a degree of fitness through the daily demands of island life, I enquired Alastair's age. He is ten years younger. Therein lies the difference, I declared. Alastair thought it might also have something to do with his radically altered consumption of alcohol. It wasn't, he said, that he was drinking less, just differently. He had forsworn stout and substituted gin and whisky. This, he averred, had made a new man of him. I made a mental note to seek verification from his "significant other".

With the help of the twins and a week-long bonfire, the invading rhododendrons were eradicated from the surface of what was now discernible as a very ample space for a single grass court. To judge from the height of the bank on the north side and the ha-ha on the south, the creation of this level space must have involved colossal redistribution of soil. The texture of the soil, with sand through it, also indicated that it had been brought from elsewhere, for it is dissimilar to the acid, boggy earth to be found anywhere else on the arable sector of this island.

Having cleared the undergrowth we could see which of the old apple trees were worth preserving and which merited replacing, before any bright spark came up with the idea of restoring a grass court in Connemara ... Kraken offered his services, strictly in a consultant's capacity. His family had grown apples commercially in Norway since the time Brian Boru spoiled their holiday in Dublin.

> "They are Norse! For the bugles are wild in the woods,
> Alarms to the farms to look after their goods:
> To bury their cauldrons and hide all their herds.
> They are Norse! I can tell by the length of their swords —"
> "High Tide at Malahide" — O. St. J. Gogarty

Kraken requested instead a saw and a crange, deploying them with a severity that made me cringe. Yet I could soon see the method in his apparent madness, for great, gangling, straggling branches were ruthlessly stripped away to trees dramatically transformed from hippies to guardsmen. Kraken declared that such treatment as this would galvanise the old trees, inducing blossom instead of simply sprouting more shoots of barren wood. Irrespective of the quality of their fruit, he claimed that the old trees would ensure the successful pollination of the new, for modern strains need more help in this regard than their rugged predecessors.

Encouraged by this reclamation of a recent wilderness, I resolved to embark on a limited replanting programme, introducing splashes of colour into what was otherwise a summer profusion of greenery, save for the roses, the buddleia and the laburnum that surrounded the lawn. This "lawn", as we called it, is a fanciful term for the area of grass and weeds between the south side of the house and the water's edge, which last summer's repeated tonsuring had tamed to a tolerable degree. At least the rushes seemed to have been subdued, though they can remain dormant for up to sixty years.

Another significant step towards civilising the outward appearance of the house—to my mind anyway—was achieved by burying the black hydrodare pipe through which the water is pumped from the lake up into the tank in the attic—a daily routine. In former summer stays down here this pipe had been simply rolled out across the lawn for the duration and then stored indoors during our absence, while the petrol-driven pump was brought ashore for servicing and winter storage. It all looked terribly temporary. An afternoon's work sufficed to bury it and thus transform the appearance of the lawn—as I thought. To my dismay, the disappearance of this black pipe aroused not a single comment, not one.

The belated arrival of spring was eventually signalled by the annual reappearance of the "tourist donkeys" in Tully village. No one seems to know where this pair hibernate, but their return to the village is greeted with weary resignation by

Donal O'Dea and anyone else attempting to infuse a little colour into the village through planting out flowers and shrubs. The donkeys hover on the village green until the dead of night, when they stealthily descend upon the sleeping village to assuage their herbiferous hunger.

Seasonal donkeys abound throughout Connemara. Some suspect that they are wintered in a vast hangar under the auspices of Bord Fáilte, released at strategic points at the beginning of each tourist season to beguile our visitors. Years of experience wandering the landscape have enabled these donkeys to distinguish between Irish-owned motorcars, hire cars and foreign-owned cars, for they will shun the first category, while shuffling up to the visitors in the expectation of tasty morsels in return for posing to be photographed.

The surviving cock pheasants, silent until now, begin calling to their opposite numbers, while the mallard around the island and the shore begin to preen themselves to get the down with which to line their nests. There is a menage-à-trois of these mallard based near the boathouse. They rise into the air, squawking high dudgeon at our approach. Interestingly, this trio comprises two drakes and one duck.

Were I still Alastair's age, I should be affronted by this apparent imbalance of nature. "Well stepped in years" now, I am less adamant upon such issues. Besides, this arrangement seems to satisfy all parties.

The sudden appearance of a pair of swans on the lake suggests another "arrangement". This merits investigation. Sure enough, on the smaller, poorer Renvyle lake we find our widowed swan keeping company with the "Chinese" goose. It is as though Tully lake is the "big house" of the swan world, and Renvyle lake the dower house, for cygnets are never seen on Renvyle lake.

The smooth course of nature on Heather Island is suddenly shattered. Milady has adopted a second cat, likewise female.

The result is chaotic. The black and white cat violently resents this intruder, a marmalade refugee from Letterfrack, where it has been rescued from a lingering demise by Mabs, the animal-lover, restored to health, and wished upon Milady. The house becomes a battleground, with each cat determined to establish its own territory by defecating therein. While a truce is declared at feeding time, all the other hours that God sends are spent in ambushing each other, mewling and spitting, tufts of hair floating in the breeze. The original cat is invariably the aggressor, but she lacks the street wisdom of the Letterfrack cat, that has eyes in the back of her head and is obviously well versed in urban guerrilla warfare. Teal and Plover are clearly bemused, as their support is courted, first by the incumbent, then by the interloper.

The arrival of spring is manifest in more than nature, for it signals the resumption of the building spree, evidence of the success of those discreet little notices that have flapped in the winds on plots all over the peninsula throughout the winter months. Barely legible, they have complied with the planning requirements that oblige intending builders to make public their proposals by way of newspaper insertions and notices on the sites in question. High on the hillsides surrounding the lake earthmoving machinery appears; the first step to clearing, levelling and draining. Infinitely more dramatic, because of its sheer size, is the extension to the Renvyle Inn, which guards the western approach to Tully village.

Michael, one of an army of artisans involved in the block-laying, informs me cheerfully that it is exactly ten years since an earlier extension was erected—and as quickly dismantled, having been put up on ground that belonged to another. These things happen. The Renvyle Inn had been Wallace's for many years, as many as I could remember and long before that too, as my mother had told me. In her childhood days in Renvyle House her parents had bought her an elderly pony, from the postman. Perfect for her needs in every other respect, this pony proved incorrigible in one regard. Accustomed over years and years to pause for a certain period of time outside Wallace's on its return journey from Renvyle when delivering and collecting the post, it stubbornly refused to relinquish that practice simply through change of ownership and usage. Humiliated by continuous failure to re-programme her recalcitrant steed, my mother resorted to subterfuge. She invented all manner of pretexts to call on the numerous shops that were in Tully in those days, while the pony grazed the village green for the time it took a thirsty postman to down a half-one and a bottle of porter.

April

The family assembled for Easter, only to go their separate ways, much, much too soon. As if in a rush to make up for a slow start to the season, tour buses and fish transporters suddenly clogged the roads, deserted until now. The turnover of tourists would continue right into the autumn, whereas this influx of salmon smolts from the hatcheries was part of a two-year cycle, which would see them fed to maturity in the cages dotted along this coast.

By one of those delightful coincidences that provide both pleasure and pain, the children's return dovetailed neatly with the belated arrival of the sycamore saplings from Belgium. These would have to be planted immediately, for they had already begun to sprout, even though the bunches of fifty each were hooded in black polythene bags. Not a moment must be lost! We lugged them over to the eastern end of the island and set to work, in teams of two; one to dig the hole, the other to install the sapling and tread the earth back firmly around the roots. Quite soon it became apparent that the quantity estimated and purchased was far, far in excess of what the area of ground could accommodate. Panic stations!

Fortunately, the notion of planting broadleaved trees seemed to strike a chord in the hearts and minds of other landowners and fellow-imbibers, for a few evening sessions in the Trading Post saw most of the surplus find new homes throughout the area. Some were to prove successful, others not. Failure was attributed to the depredations of the Houdini-like deer, supposedly confined to the National Park.

The depredations of the deer were only trifling compared to the Good Friday night sabotage of the salmon cages in Mannin Bay. The destruction of these cages and the consequent release of 250,000 salmon smolts into the waters of the Atlantic represented a future loss of one million pounds. A spokesman for the Salmon Growers' Association likened this action to the burning down of a factory. Connemara "enjoyed" national media coverage that it could happily have done without and suddenly the whole issue had pierced the surface of local society, poisoning the atmosphere. Anonymous, cowardly, threatening telephone calls became the order of the day, polarising and paralyzing.

Subsequent sightings of enormous schools of dolphins close by the shores may not have been unconnected with the happenings in Mannin Bay. But to those not embroiled in the "fish war", as it had been dubbed, the dolphins were harbingers of a hot summer, something seldom seen in Connemara in recent years. Their appearance in such numbers and so close inshore gave rise to all sorts of dolphin stories.

One concerned a dolphin jumping into an anchored currach, giving birth before the eyes of the astonished crew, while the other dolphins jostled the boat. Collecting their scattered wits, the fishermen scooped up both mother and baby and heaved them overboard, whereupon the other dolphins began tossing the baby high in the air with their spouts, as if in celebration of its birth.

Any fishy story inevitably begets another. The sequel recounted how the Killary school of dolphins had frequently been observed tossing wild salmon high into the air several times before devouring their prey, just as a cat will play with a mouse. When called upon for expert comment, neither Batman nor Gerry Park would be drawn into the mischievous conclusion that dolphins eat their offspring.

Back on Tully Lake a different form of fish liberation took place, on a boiling hot day, as luck would have it. A 'phone call alerted me to be ready for the arrival of some two hundred well-grown brown trout from the hatchery in Cong. Once again, time would be of the essence. A speedy transfer from tank to lake was vital. Alastair and Geoffrey and Batman responded to my pleas for help. Using two boats, with barrels and buckets, we accomplished the distribution of these gleaming specimens over as large an area as we could row. While one pulled on the oars, the other scooped three or four fish at a time from the swaying barrel and decanted them with silvered splashes into the waters of the lake. How would these relative giants adapt to the acid waters of their new habitat? Only time would show.

Unable to resist the temptation, Nicholas and I went fishing towards dusk, curious to see what reaction there might be to the sudden invasion of these big stockies, for trout are essentially territorial. It had worked a treat. The native populace had been thoroughly stirred up, rising to our flies with a vigour not seen in years. Inevitably, we caught a couple of the new arrivals, accustomed as they had been to devouring anything that landed on the surface of their feeding ponds in Cong. Further curiosity led us to cook, consume and compare the old with the new. There was no comparison. The natives were pink-fleshed, firm and succulent, whereas the arrivistes were white-fleshed, flaccid and tasteless. They would need time to adapt and then adjust to life in the wild, where regular meals were not assured.

Unlike the herons that had begun to reoccupy what had traditionally been called Heron Island, the pair of swans were unmoved by all this fish business, for they live on plant life from the lake bed. They had begun to show signs of settling on the same little islet that swans have always and ever nested upon whenever cygnets had been hatched here. Returning one morning from delivering Milady ashore, I watched the swans confront each other in the water, rising up vertically, their necks entwined, making moaning sounds, in what must surely have been a courtship ritual. It was a remarkable sight; these stately, almost supercilious creatures carrying on like us lower orders.

Easter brought the first influx of regular visitors to Connemara, the ones who maintain holiday houses, some as a fishing base and others simply to enjoy their surroundings, for there is no place quite like Connemara. You can lose your very soul to this place.

> "The lanes that end on hill or strand
> Of this, the Many Coloured Land,
> Are dearer than the burdened roads
> That cross the Lands of Many Loads."
>
> "Connemara" — Oliver St John Gogarty

This welcome return of seasonal neighbours brought Simon McCormick, complete with his Bunnaboghee house party from Dublin, and further afield. They would pay us a call, around lunchtime. And this they duly did, bearing bags of oysters, bottles of wine and — to cap it all — four or five local lobsters, cooked and cold; "to accompany the salad, don't you see!" Rising to the spirit of the occasion, the weather gods poured sun down from cloudless skies, as garden furniture, interred since last year, was hastily assembled on the lawn to receive this feast.

Milady was in her element, playing hostess to this cosmopolitan company, whose careers took them all over the world, enabling them to converse upon all those faraway places with strange-sounding names she yearns to see. The lake glistened in the sunshine. The thrushes and the blackbirds sang on cue and Heather Island was as Heather Island is meant to be—a summer wonderland.

However, this year the summer season on Heather Island assumed a completely different perspective—to me at least. In previous years we had descended as and when the fancy took us, cobbled the old place together on a wing and a prayer and hoped it stayed fine. Now it was our home. We had wintered here (well, for the most part) and everything had had time to settle in and find its place. No more those frantic searches for the corkscrew. It now had its appointed place—righthand front drawer of the kitchen dresser. True, an awful lot remained to be done. But so it would be, all in good time, freed as we were now from the constraints of a lost weekend now and a frenetic fortnight again. It helped, too, that Heather Island was now our only residence, unrivalled by permanent abodes in Tullamore or Yorkshire, which had always claimed priority through greater occupation.

Just as the old house had responded to being lived in, as opposed to invaded by holidaying hordes for brief backwoodsmen's carousings—"They lived and loved and laughed and left"—so too the grounds. They were beginning, anyway, to show signs of being tended, whereas in the past they had been attacked to curtail the encroachment of undergrowth and jungle, intent on smothering the old house, reducing it to a toppled ruin, a pale imitation of the tumbled temples of Peru.

To retreat into reverie on occasions such as this impromptu garden lunch party can be a useful ploy, as others, noting their host's abstracted state, may be moved to grapple with the opening of the oysters. This is a potentially maiming exercise and is not advised in conjunction with the consumption of alcohol. It was Benjamin, the international banker, who brought me back to the present by lamenting the absence of Guinness to wash down those oysters, particularly in Oliver

St John Gogarty's house. This man's knowledge is disconcertingly diverse. He reminded me of Gogarty's lengthy tribute to Guinness in As I was going down Sackville Street.

"... there is the great brewery that has done more for Dublin than any of its institutions. It cleared the foetid liberties long before philanthropists took to improving the houses of the poor. It provided one of the loveliest 'volks garten' in Europe, and it set the model to employers long before Henry Ford expounded his theory of high wages. It went beyond that, for what happens in the U.S.A. to employees after the wage-earning age? —too old at forty: in Guinness you are in your prime ... if I were beginning life again I would seek a job in the brewery. I have often longed not only to take, but to make drink. And by making Guinness you make so many other things as well—garden villages, dependable workers and the 'brew that savours of content.' like dark sleep, it knits up the ravelled sleeve of care, and, what is an achievement, it wastes the time that might, if we were not drinking, be devoted to scheming, posing, hypocrisy and money-making.

"The silted Nile mouths and the Moeritic Lake": Clouds. What a wonderful communion Guinness provides! You can drink yourself into helping the poor by better housing; you can drink yourself into St. Stephen's Green, or at least into appreciation of those who gave it to the city; and you can, if you like, drink yourself into poverty and become an object, if not a dispenser of charity ... Drink to the Lord Ardilaun who gave us the Green. Drink until you see the ducks swimming in your tankard. Drink your liver into martyrdom ... take your time: there are no Neros here."

Having exposed the succulent contents of Galway Bay's finest oysters, Simon joined our company, delighted at this literary endorsement of his own personal crusade. After lengthy deliberation Simon calculated that he might well have restored St. Patrick's Cathedral singlehanded, before embarking on the renovation of the Hop Store. Impressed by his friend's munificence, Benjamin promptly enrolled as a member of the Gogarty Society, offering his services as our guide and mentor when the Society should get organised to travel to Buenos Aires in search of descendants of Gogarty's mysterious brother.

Richard Howard Aloysius Gogarty had emigrated to Argentina in the early years of this century, as Gogarty related in a letter to his son, Noll, in 1953. "So Uncle Dick has written ... He is the only brother I have left, the youngest and the only one who was not given a profession or sent to an University. He left Dublin about forty years ago in a red shirt to seek his fortune in the Argentine. His idea of it then was as a cowboy. The last I heard of him he was working for Cook's." In his new life this former Dublin agent for the Argyll Motor Company had styled himself Señor Ricardo O'Gogarty.

That Richard Gogarty had descendants we knew, for a Dermot St. John Gogarty had come to light in his role as headmaster of a boys' school near London. When asked to fill in the missing links, he had proved evasive, reluctant to elaborate on his immediate South American antecedents. There was something increasingly fantastical about a discussion such as this taking place on an island in the middle of a lake in Connemara, as remote in many ways from Ballinasloe as it is from Buenos Aires.

This sense of unreality recurred soon afterwards, following a very pleasant dinner in Renvyle House with the owners of Quigley's Farm, the pink-painted double cottage down near Gurteen pier that features in so many panoramic photographs of Killary and Muilrea. We were leaving the diningroom when a very agitated woman confronted Milady and me, brandishing coloured photographs. Were we not the owners of that house on the island near here, she demanded. Well, yes, we were ... "Were these taken on your island?" she wanted to know, and did we recognise the woman in them? Affirmative on both counts. Now what? "The man with that woman is my husband!"

The situation was becoming tricky, for this was no case of mistaken identity. The photographs, taken in the "little court paved with irregular slats, russet and brown and sea-green" clearly showed Milady, myself and "that woman", an old friend of ours, separated for many years. But of the photographer there was no sign. He had wisely taken all the pictures himself. So how had his distraught spouse come upon this "damning" evidence? She had found this roll of undeveloped film among his belongings, and taken it to the chemist's shop, and duly received the prints. That was how ...

Wearying suddenly of her sleuthing, she declared that her mother had been a diva, hence her own distinctly operatic name. It wasn't prima donna, but it could have been. She launched into one of her own compositions, which appeared to derive its inspiration equally from Christy Moore, Mary Coughlan and Michael D. Higgins. We smiled and fled. The eclectic composition of the clientele in Renvyle House ensures unexpected encounters, though seldom as bizarre as this.

The kindly couple from Quigley's Farm professed themselves intrigued. They come out to Connemara for peace and quiet, content to enjoy the environment, even if the social scene might be lacking in stimulus. Charmed and alarmed, they realised now that life in Connemara was anything but dull. Rather did it make their own, day-to-day, inland existence appear humdrum in comparison. They were being self-deprecatory, I knew. The husband, a solicitor, had been lolling at the back of a courthouse not too long before, waiting resignedly for his particular cases to come before the judge. A young man was being remanded on a triple murder charge. He was offered free legal aid and asked if he had a solicitor in mind. To our friend's dismay, the youth pointed to him. "Ah, your honour, I am not on the free legal aid panel, your honour."

"Well, you are now!"

Seventeen time-consuming and unrewarding court appearances ensued before the tormented youth had sacked our friend, in one of those fits of rage that many feared would see him found "guilty but insane". Our friend's views on his ex-client's guilt he kept to himself, quite properly. On the question of the youth's sanity he had no doubts. Twelve "just men and true" subsequently confirmed his assessment.

More recently still, our friend had hastened from the stands to the winner's enclosure to welcome his horse after a noteworthy success, confidently anticipated. Surrounded by wellwishers and elated by this long-awaited proof that his expensive purchase had justified both money and patience, he wondered at the lengthy delay ... Suddenly, an ambulance drove swiftly off the course, siren wailing, lights flashing. Our friend's winner had dropped dead on his way back to unsaddle, giving the jockey a crashing fall through the rails. This man may insist that his life is dull, but he is one of those to whom things have a habit of happening.

Our next "happening" was to be the performance of Gerry Conneely's and Philip Sweeney's dramatisation of "Sackville Street" in Dunguaire, as part of Andy Dolan's Fleadh na gCuach. It wasn't easy to get an idea of what form this staging might take. The reason—I later discovered—was that Gerry hadn't yet written the script. Sometimes ignorance is indeed bliss.

In the meantime nature took its wondrous course in and around Tully lake. The resident mallard duly hatched their clutches and were to be seen bobbing on the waves shepherding their broods, mother mallard invariably giving one of the ducklings a ride on her broad back. And our first cuckoo arrived, always a welcome sign of summer being only around the corner. Alas, the novelty of our male's constant calling soon turned to exasperation. This character worked overtime, day and night. In the daytime he would range in the hills around the lake, which was easy on the ear and pleasant to hear. But at night the so-and-so would move on to the island, seeming to perch close to our bedroom windows, where he would start up his monotonous appeals for a mate at any and all hours of darkness. I was sorely tempted to shoot him.

Actually, there's a case to be made for at least limiting the numbers of these summer visitors to our shores. Each female lays between fifteen and twenty-five eggs, all in different "host" nests. Her offspring then kill all the host bird's chicks, either by throwing the eggs out of the nest, or by murdering the chicks as soon as they hatch—hence "cuckoo in the nest". Heather Island is not that well served with songbirds and the lethal intervention of these cuckoos will do nothing to improve that situation.

To add to the racket of this twenty-four hour, round-the-clock cuckoo, Teal began barking furiously in the night, though at different times. Whatever was getting her excited seemed to be somewhere in the vicinity of the orchard, where our clearing had revealed what looked like an otter's "holt", as this nocturnal fish-killer's lair is called. While we hadn't seen an otter on the island for years, we knew they lived here, for their paths to the lakeshore were kept open through regular use.

Just how quiet and deserted Heather Island had become in the 'fifties was indicated by an otter raising her two cubs in an overturned tea chest under the veranda, just by the hall door. On our arrival for that summer's holidays this shy creature had disappeared, abandoning her cubs. In our attempts to become surrogate mother to these waifs, we did the wrong thing, diluting cows' milk when we should have fortified it. When, inevitably, the cubs died, the local postman cured the pelts, which adorned my sister's coat collars for many years afterwards.

One morning, after a particularly noisy night, Teal was in bits, bleeding profusely from her head and ears. As springers don't tangle with rats, we assumed that her opponent had been an otter. If this were so then Teal was foolish, for a dog otter generally weighs 20–25 lbs., while they have been recorded as weighing up to 40lbs. Plover looked quite smugly at Milady's fussing over the tattered Teal, for Plover values her night's sleep on the wrecked chaise longue on the veranda. No nocturnal escapades for her.

A few nights later, I went down to the pier as the light faded to see whether there mightn't be a late rise of trout, for it just seemed that sort of night when a late foray on to the lake can yield the following night's dinner. The dogs followed me. Something barely breaking the surface of the lake caught my eye. It caught Teal's too, for she began yapping furiously. Only yards away this big otter was swimming quite unconcernedly. Blithely disregarding his adversary's barking, he swam over to the little island just north of the main island, his huge, flat tail just visible below the surface. Reaching the shore, he or she— for I could not tell—climbed ashore and disappeared into the undergrowth. Teal made a very half-hearted attempt to give chase, and doubled quickly back up to the house. Case closed.

At this time of year, before the foliage reaches its full density, we can see the church in Tullycross from the east-facing kitchen window and thus we could see it suddenly covered in scaffolding. What could be happening to the Church of Christ the King, with its renowned Harry Clarke stained-glass windows behind the altar, donated by old Mrs. Gogarty and her brother in their parents' memory? My parents had been married in this church, my father buried from it and our daughter, Rebecca, baptised there. It was in more ways than one a landmark in our lives. We needn't have worried. Far from being in imminent danger of collapse, the church was getting a facelift for the forthcoming Confirmation, which takes place in Tullycross every few years, on a rotation throughout the parish.

The ceremony whereby teenagers become confirmed as "Soldiers of Christ" is a milestone in their young spiritual lives. It is also an occasion of communal celebration, in which the entire parish becomes involved. Having lived away for years, we had forgotten just what an occasion Confirmation is, presided over by the bishop of Tuam no less. The whole exterior was steam cleaned, the guttering replaced and the entire building then repainted, standing out more prominently than before, dominating the landscape for miles in every direction.

On the day itself the three villages, Tully, Tullycross and Letterfrack were festooned in bunting. It was as though a local holiday had been declared, which—if you take holiday as "Holy Day"—indeed it had. At mid-morning Tullycross became impassable for cars parked and latterly just abandoned. When the lengthy ceremony ended the throng of cars and their full complements spread throughout the three villages; the collective mood switching now from spiritual to social, then to convivial and later to loquacious. What, I wondered, had our anthropologists from Aquinas College made of it all, looking on through the windows of the thatched cottages in Tullycross?

Come to think of it, the anthropologists missed another glorious opportunity to observe the Irish psyche in the raw in Kinvara, at the Fleadh na gCuach. One of the earlier events in the summer-long calendar of festivals all over Ireland, the Cuckoo Festival had started two days and two nights before the scheduled staging of "Sackville Street" in Dunguaire. Winkle's Hotel looked as though it had hosted the Battle of Aughrim and Andy Dolan was nowhere to be found. "Try around the pubs. You're sure to find him, in one or another!"

"One or another" turned out to be close on twenty, for Kinvara is one of those villages, common throughout this country, where virtually every building is a licensed premises. This phenomenon has its origins in the Penal Laws, which forbade a Catholic ownership of anything other than a public house, or a horse valued at less than five pounds. When taken to the letter of the law, these iniquitous strictures obliged a Catholic horseman to surrender his steed to any member of the Established Church prepared to proffer five pounds on the spot. The Penal laws were repealed in the aftermath of the French Revolution, and have stealthily been replaced by an ecumenical tyranny entitled Offences against the Road Traffic Act.

Andy Dolan's trail turned hot and cold by turn, for he appeared to have bestowed his custom on every one of these numerous hostelries, doubtless in his capacity as prime mover of the Cuckoo Festival. The custodians of each inn were perplexed: "You're sure to see him about the place. 'T'isn't Dublin yer in now."

"Grand. But how will I know him?" Welcomes turned to hostility. Who was this stranger looking for Andy but unable to recognise their unofficial lord mayor? Was he a taxman, a bailiff, a gripper?

"Ah, now … you'll know him right enough." Judas has no cousins in Kinvara.

A bellowed challenge from a burly, barrel-chested character striding down the middle of the main street solved my dilemma. The jungle drums had sped the word of warning, turning the tables. The pursuer had become the pursued. Thus did Andy Dolan find me.

We made our stately way across the head of the harbour to Dunguaire in a jalopy that defied all the conventions ever enshrined in the Offences against the Road Traffic Act. It could have come to Kinvara by way of Hongkong, Macau and mainland China, but it would never make Connemara, the final resting place for so many of its ilk. Gerry and Philip, resplendent in blazers and boaters, were rehearsing their parts in the courtyard of the castle. They had extrapolated all the political harangues and diatribes that run throughout "Sackville Street", with particular emphasis on Northern Ireland ...

The candlelit theatre on the middle floor of the castle is small enough to create an immediate intimacy between actors and audience. Onlookers become conspirators. And so it was for the next forty, captivating, enthralling minutes, as Gerry and then Philip continually reversed roles, becoming in turn Gogarty, Griffith, Collins, de Valera and even Carson. Gerry's fascination with Irish politics came shining through as he declaimed the passages that explained just why the notion of an Ireland united was just that — a notion, a whimsy, an impractical fantasy. *As I was going down Sackville Street* was published in 1937. The obstacles to a united Ireland, as Gogarty outlined them then, remain. So Conor Cruise O'Brien had recently acknowledged.

Jan Voske joined in the pleasurable post-mortem on Connolly's pub overlooking the harbour. Thoroughly into the spirit of the Cuckoo Festival, Jan waxed lyrically about the variety of musical talent gathered in Kinvara for the occasion. He particularly enthused about "Some Like It Hot", whom we knew well, for these demonic musicians live in Eagles' Nest, barely a mile to the west of Tully Lake. Then there was "Begley and Cooney", "Bill Carson and Killer Kane", "The Lahanns" and the "Máimín Cajun Band". "Sure, you can't leave now. When you've hardly even arrived!"

Milady was adamant, citing a dozen pressing reasons for a speedy withdrawal. Hers was the last word on the matter! Once again feminine intuition was proved right. At our next breakfast board meeting in Renvyle House, Jan did not appear. Smiling his rueful smile, Prince Hal bade Falstaff recount the reason. In appropriately solemn tones, this "lover of sack and jests" narrated the saga of the near-immolation of East Germany's finest. Full of "the water of life" the painter of pretty posters had retired to his mobile home, lit a candle by which to read in bed, and promptly succumbed in the arms of Morpheus. A breeze blew up, wafting the curtains gently over the flaming candle. Waking to find his curtains ablaze, the artist succeeded in extinguishing the flames with his bare hands. Staggering out into the night air to avoid suffocation, he trod, barefoot, on the shattered remains of a bottle that had slipped from his grasp and broken in the course of his tortuous return home.

Falstaff could contain his mirth no longer, rolling around in glee at the vision of an artist without the use of his hands. Prince Hal was less amused, for he had already advanced a considerable proportion of the fee for a commission which now appeared forfeit ... His bacon and sausage and black pudding and tomatoes and fried egg coagulated and congealed as he pondered — more like Shylock now — how to wrest his pound of flesh from this defaulter with neither hands nor feet.

Mopping his brow, and then his plate, Falstaff remembered his role: "I am not only witty in myself, but the cause that wit is in other men". He murmured the dreaded words: "Renvyle Hydrilla". Prince Hal's countenance brightened instantly; the storm clouds rolled back; the sun shone. "Yes! Excellent Sir John. Why no reference to our hydrilla in the manuscript. Did you not receive the paper on it from the Botanic Gardens in Glasnevin?"

Glasnevin would have been just the place for Falstaff, I

thought: a fried Friar Tuck, in a little urn. They waited. How was the scribe going to answer this charge? Attack seemed the only form of defence. "The hydrilla has vanished, Bottom says. It's disappeared. Evaporated. Vamoosed. When the sea washed into the lake during the storm the salt killed it." The Prince fixed his manager with that dreaded basilisk stare. Bottom quailed, automatically accepting full responsibility for the storm, the flooding of the lake by the sea and the disappearance of the hydrilla. The pupils of his eyes swivelled sharply inwards, threatening to vanish behind the bridge of his nose. A career move loomed large ...

Scowling now, Prince Hal silently thrust a paper across the boardroom table to Falstaff, who hastily finished the toast, swallowed his coffee and cleared his throat in preparation. "The Renvyle Hydrilla," he began, "a submerged aquatic monocotyledon, previously unknown in Ireland, was recorded in 1935 from Rusheenduff, a small lake in the grounds of Renvyle Hotel, separated from the sea only by a shingle bar ... A delicate, light green, perennial, underwater herb, glabrous and smooth, apparently dioecious, dying down in winter and regenerating the following year, partly from dormant winter buds and partly from bulbil-like buds which terminate stolons buried in the substratum. Stem erect up to 37 cm long in cultivation, very slender terete, usually reddish, freely branched near the base, the branches being often of comparable length to the main stem and thus pseudo-dichotomous ..."

Prince Hal lifted a languid hand. He had heard enough. If Bottom had, indeed, lost the Renvyle Hydrilla, Bottom had lost his bonus, if not his job, for this was not the first faux pas. There had been that business with the rooster and the American lady, in addition to those unfortunate Germans, ambushed by "Nazis" on the very avenue of "Ireland's only stress-free zone" ...

April

The American lady, coming as she did from the Bronx, was terrified by the strange sounds of the countryside, and not at all reassured on being told that the crowing of the Renvyle cockerel merely denoted the dawning of another (rainy) day in Connemara. Three times she had demanded to be moved to another bedroom. On the third occasion Bottom had issued an ultimatum to his harassed lieutenant, Oswald: "That bloody bird goes, or you do!" It's known as "incentive management".

Having got the loan of an ancient, pump-action shotgun, Oswald spent a sleepless night to ensure that the Bronx lady enjoyed an uninterrupted sojourn in feather island. As the first streaks of dawn crept over Renvyle, so our intrepid assassin crept around close to the walls of the sleeping hotel. He froze. The cockerel was perched on the roof of the greenhouse. It flapped his wings, stretched skywards and opened its beak. Oswald fired. His aim was low. Glass flew everywhere. Murderous now, Oswald gave chase, firing again as the cockerel fled across the croquet lawn, and again as his quarry squawked past the putting green and into the cover of the shrubbery, and again on the off-chance, until the magazine was empty.

Oswald, the frustrated assassin, retreated indoors to find the hallway jammed with frightened guests in their nightwear. "What in God's name's goin' on around here! Is it a raid? Is it a robbery? Hey! Don't shoot, mister! We ain't done nothin'." Bottom was implacable. Oswald got the DCM. So did the cockerel—strangled.

The Nazi business had been nobody's fault really, more a misunderstanding. Some nationalities take everything at face value, even in Connemara. It had been another of those exceptionally popular "Murder, Mystery Weekends". Then this carload of elderly Germans arrived in the middle of it all, not knowing the score. Well, of course they had scrambled out of the car with their hands in the air, jabbering in terror, before

173

the actors in Nazi uniform realised that these belated arrivals couldn't have been aware of the game plan. Dr. Desdemona had been livid, claiming that cardiac arrest could so easily have resulted. Worse still, *The Irish Times* had run the story. Prince Hal had sent a note to Bottom: "All the world's a stage, and all the men and women merely players: they have their exits ..."

Vowing to fight fire with fire, Bottom resolved to reply in similarly erudite vein.

> "When daisies pied and violets blue
> And lady-smocks all silver-white
> And cuckoo buds of yellow hue
> Do paint the meadows with delight,
> The cuckoo then, on every tree,
> Mocks married men; for thus sings he,
> Cuckoo; cuckoo, cuckoo; O, word of fear,
> Unpleasing to a married ear!"

Mariana, veteran of many such crises in the "stress-free zone", counselled restraint: "He uses his folly like a stalking-horse, and under the presentation of that he shoots his wit."

May

"May's fairest flowers" excelled themselves this year, lighting up the landscape in a blaze of yellow gorse, counterpointed by the suffused purples of the rhododendron, that added colour where none had existed up the flanks of the Twelve Bens Heather Island had become a patchwork quilt of primroses and bluebells, interspersed with the odd clump of whitebells (if that is the term for white bluebells). The flowering cherry trees spread ethereal canopies of pink and white, while Kraken's tonsuring had revived the old apple trees, just as he had predicted. Malachy Kane's observation seemed to be coming true: "If you want to turn this old place around, the only way you'll do it is by living here."

On days of flat calm the surface of the lake reflected the blazing gorse bushes as if the very depths of the lake itself were on fire. The sycamore saplings duly sprouted their modest clusters of leaves, waving dottily in the breeze, while, on the lawn, the medlar tree put out sprays of delicate white blossom, that would later turn to fruit, edible when decayed. The blueberry bushes, responding gratefully to the absence of herbivores, promised a bumper crop. From a lattice of bare trunks and branches, the trees that define the island's outline gradually transformed into one huge, green umbrella, punctuated here and there by dark blotches of copper beech. Already it was becoming difficult to recreate in the mind's eye the bleak and barren winter scene. The surrounding hillsides moved slowly from grey and brown, drab and drear, to smiling green, dotted with sheep and lambs; winter morasses closed away now for summer meadows.

Our own timidity in the gardening sphere was brought home to me each midday, as I took the dogs to the village to collect the post and the newspapers. This necessitated passing Thady Hurley's neat and fertile garden in which he was always to be found, sowing this, weeding that. One day my greeting met a rueful response. "D'ye see what the bleddy badger's after doin'? Every last one o' me carrots, the beggar's after devourin'." Sure enough, the once-neat bed was pitted now with regular rows of holes, from which the badger had expertly extracted the fledgling carrots. "And it must've been the badger, for no dog would be bothered with the likes o' thim." I looked at Plover: she looked away.

Thady lived for his garden, backing the odd horse on an English racecourse; a retrospective tribute to a working life spent over the Irish Sea. Thady could have found his way around London blindfolded, whereas Dublin was a foreign city, alien to Connemara men. As we chatted about this and that—racing mostly—it occurred to me that not even Dick Francis at his most inventive could have devised the death that Thady had so narrowly avoided.

He had been fencing his garden one day, using lengths of barbed wire, to deter roaming livestock from invading the most inviting garden for miles around. The length of wire he was working with happened to trail across the laneway, in the path of a passing car. The end of the wire got wrapped around the axle of the car, while the middle of it encircled Thady ... Mercifully, the driver realised and reacted, though not before poor Thady had been dragged down the lane and almost sliced into several sections, as the rapidly tightening loops cut through his sparse flesh to the very bone.

This near-tragedy I had heard at second hand, for it is not something one would readily bring up in conversation with the hapless victim in person. Instead Thady mused about the forthcoming County Fleadh coming to Tully and Tullycross and the wondrous transformation of the Renvyle Inn in readiness for the great occasion. From where we stood we could see the army of artisans finishing the roof, extending and levelling the carpark, breaking out doors where once had been windows and ferrying in all the paraphernalia of a restaurant.

The coming of the County Fleadh—the Galway finals of competitions in all aspects of Irish music and dancing—represented a major coup for our two villages, and a personal triumph for Michael O'Neill, the tireless headmaster of Eagle's Nest primary school. Michael seems able to cram more hours into his working day than others manage to pack into an entire week. His big, navy Volvo is a familiar sight on the roads of Connemara, serving as transport, office and political clinic, in his other capacity as County Councillor.

At the opposite end of Tully village, Golden's pub sprouted an "outdoor disco and open-air bar-b-que", to entertain the anticipated hordes of singers, dancers, musicians and camp-followers from all over this far-flung county. Meanwhile, Letterfrack distanced itself from this prospect of bacchanalian revelry, since it did not stand to benefit directly. Instead the talk was of the fish farming protest march through the streets of Clifden, with endless speculation on the outcome of the "fish war". As if all of this upheaval were not enough at the outset of a promising tourist season, the age-old stasis and inertia of clique-ridden Clifden had been shattered by the announcement of an impending Holiday Inn. What next, for heaven's sake! The airport had been repelled, albeit narrowly, and only after a long struggle by the "No surrender" rump. Now those lunatics in Brussels were talking about reviving the railway, again. It would only cost £24m.

That passing reference to the old Galway–Clifden railway line, closed with indecent haste in 1935, instilled pangs of guilt in this would-be chronicler of its brief but colourful history. Had I not vowed to walk its 49-mile trail from Galway to Clifden station, which still stands, in the site of the threatened Holiday Inn? "Ilea jacta est!" Perhaps Pete could be persuaded to accompany me on the odyssey. Frederick Norton Peters consented, decent man that he is.

Whimsically, we decided to conduct our campaign in stages, determined by the existence of watering-holes along our route. We would do the last stage first; logically we averred, for this gave us Ballynahinch Castle as our refuge, halfway between Recess and Clifden. Armed with Tim Robinson's invaluable map of Connemara and a sufficiency of cigarettes, we headed off the beaten path and into the wilds between Loch Atrai and Loch na Brocai (the lake of the badger's den). We did not take J. H. Ryan's Paper, read to the Institute of Engineers of Ireland in 1901, in which the railway is described in meticulous detail. This proved no great loss, for many of the features outlined therein no longer exist, among them "Bridge No. 23, at 37¾ miles, is 20 feet span, and carries the railway over a small river." Its disappearance necessitated fording the "small river"—easy enough, once resigned to getting our feet wet.

Our route took us through the spectacular cutting behind Lisnabrucka. Amongst the Lawrence Collection of photographs in the National Library is a particularly evocative picture of the construction crew in the process of drilling this awesome feature of the line, without any of the machinery considered indispensable by ESB crews in modern times. The marks of their drills remain starkly imprinted upon the sides of the cutting. Beyond lies the "new" cemetery, known locally as Hynes' Park. The name commemorates a long-dead proprietor of the eating house and shebeen at this point on the ancient bridle-path to Ballynahinch. From open countryside we plunged into the dense pine forests that lead the way to Ballynahinch Castle, historic home of the Martins, the largest landowners in these islands.

Today Ballynahinch is a pleasant, welcoming country house hotel, its reputation founded on the legendary salmon fishing in the river below the old house. The bar—more English than Irish in ambience—is a very easy place in which to while away those hours, "that might, if we were not drinking, be devoted to scheming, posing, hypocrisy and money-making." Even the daft, imaginary likeness of Graunaile, looking dolefully into an empty tankard becomes an object of amusement rather than derision, as the Guinness soothes both mind and body.

Tempted though we were to relive those long, leisurely sessions in distant Yorkshire, the prospect of the second phase of our pilgrimage loomed large and menacing. The barman wished us luck, carefully noncommittal between the courage or contrariness of our venture. We still had nine miles to traverse to Clifden, with no watering-hole to sustain us on our way.

The remains of the level-crossing gates are still to be seen where the line passed from Ballynahinch station on its final stage to Clifden, a stage which began with the 50 ft. span across the Cloonbeg river, which is still passable, with care. The lush vegetation surrounding Ballynahinch abruptly gives way to vast expanses and limitless horizons of rock and bog, lakes and distant hills; the old railbed the only mark of mankind upon this desolate terrain.

Skylarks were our only company and in this uninhabited tract—for all the world like a green-grey desert—we found ample evidence of the indecent haste with which the rails had been ripped up, carted into Clifden and loaded on to a German freighter in Clifden port. Here we found a fishplate, there a dog-spike and further on a four-fang bolt. Soon we had more ironmongery than it was comfortable to carry, souvenirs of that wanton act of vandalism committed sixty years ago.

As we neared the final stretch into Clifden we came upon the ruins of Munga Lodge, once the home of one of the most colourful adventurers in Clifden's chequered history—one Moreton Frewen. His exploits are recorded in an aptly titled biography, *The Splendid Pauper*. Born in 1853 and educated at Cambridge, Moreton Frewen had taken just three years to dissipate a substantial inheritance, on gambling, fox-hunting, horse-racing and lavish entertainment of the opposite sex—"a man after my own heart", we volunteered as one. The outcome of a race on Friday 13 September 1878 was chosen as the medium to determine this sportsman's future. If the horse won, Moreton Frewen would become a Master of Foxhounds. If it lost, he would emigrate to Wyoming, "a territory he had never seen and knew only as an Indian battlefield".

The race on which Frewen's future depended was the Doncaster Cup. Whatever carried his money, it can't have been the winning favourite, Pageant, ridden by the redoubtable Tom Cannon, distant forebear of Lester Piggott. Persuading his brother, Richard, to join him in a ranching venture, Moreton Frewen sold up, borrowed all he could and emigrated, setting up the largest spread in Wyoming, extending from "the Rawhide near two hundred miles east, to Tongue River, a hundred miles north". He married Clara Jerome, daughter of New York millionaire Leonard Jerome and elder sister of Winston Churchill's mother, Jennie Jerome. At its zenith the Frewen ranch carried nearly seventy thousand head of cattle and employed seventy-five cowboys. Sadly, a series of reverses were destined to bankrupt the intrepid Moreton Frewen, along with the rest of his family.

Back in the halcyon days of Munga Lodge the Galway— Clifden train would make an unscheduled stop abreast of the lodge, allowing house guests to alight in eager anticipation of the revelries for which their hosts were renowned. Today the ruined remains of Munga Lodge stand in silent salute to the forlorn railway embankment.

Between us and our destination lay Waterloo Bridge, by-passed now, but until recent times the main road bridge into the town of Clifden from the Galway direction. On its day of days—Sunday, 17 September 1843—Waterloo Bridge was crossed by the greatest crowd ever to assemble in Clifden. The occasion was one of Daniel O'Connell's "Monster Meetings", through which he sought to achieve Repeal of the Act of Union, by peaceful means. The crowds that descended upon Clifden for this rally was estimated at one hundred thousand. How many of this multitude were destined to perish in the impending Famine?

Tired but triumphant, we slaked our considerable thirst in E. J. King's, congratulating ourselves on having accomplished a full quarter of the railway line's entire length. And had we had any inkling at all of the horrors that lay in wait along the remaining threequarters, we should have declared the whole escapade closed.

Our eventual return to base fortuitously involved a call into the Trading Post, where quite extraordinary goings-on were to be observed—from the sanctuary of a nigh-empty bar. It seemed that every able-bodied male throughout the length and breadth of the Renvyle peninsula had answered the call for volunteers to collect up all the "dead" cars and vans and tractors that had for so long been a feature of the local landscape. As we watched, amazed, queues of living trucks and tractors with trailers wound their way on to the waste land beside the Trading Post, off-loading wrecks of every make and shape, many unidentifiable so advanced was their decomposition. In no time they covered an acre of ground. Some days later, when the clean-up was declared complete, the Galway Metal Company crushed and drew away 320 tons of scrap metal.

Such was the fervour engendered by the neighbourhood's response, those whose motor vehicles had begun to exhibit signs of terminal decline were careful to transfer their custom for the duration, lest these zealots might be tempted to add still-serviceable vehicles to this auto-da-fé. As it was, those who failed to heed the warning sign, "No Spares", found it in their hearts to return their prizes; under cover of darkness, of course. Concern was voiced for the future of farmyard poultry on the peninsula, for it was universally agreed that every Connemara hen spent much of her life in what was once the family car. It wasn't just about poultry either. Looking at people gazing at these rusted remains of what had once upon a time been somebody's pride and joy we wondered, idly, about the number of lives that had ended — and begun — in these relics of the motor age.

A sufficiency of Guinness, imbibed thoughtfully, in congenial surroundings, in Connemara, in summer, after a laudable day's labour, can inspire the loftiest of philosophical conjecture. Joined now by Kraken — philosopher and epicurean — we became immersed in consideration of the character traits that could be attributed to being conceived in a Ford Fiesta or an Opel Kadett, as distinct from feather island ... Would the progeny of such a coupling be restless in character, lacking a sense of place and permanence, or merely mechanically-minded? Kraken took the view that such children would be imbued with a wanderlust, driven by an impulse they could not understand and their mothers might never explain, to roam the countries and even the oceans of the globe. I could see his gist, for Kraken had recently spent a year at sea. Pete reserved his opinion, muttering that a stretch limo or, better still, a Hiace van would be required were he to conduct such an experiment.

Batman's appearance in our midst was a signal to return to more material matters. Had we seen that incitement to murder and mayhem in today's paper? The seals. Yer man recommended going after them with 1914 Enfields, or Bren guns, for God's sake! Kraken became instantly businesslike. The coast of Norway had been devastated by voracious seals that had crossed from Canada, having wiped out the Canadian fishing grounds. Seals were a scourge, a menace, to be eliminated! Batman produced the relevant piece. Sure enough, an ex-chairman of the North Western Fishery Board called for a massive cull of seals, advocating a return to the good old days when it was legal to kill seals and suggesting that the Army might be better deployed shooting seals than firing at stationary targets. Well, we knew where Batman stood on this issue. Hadn't that seal with its death wish nearly hastened him to an early grave?

Pete perused this extraordinary epistle and grew pensive. He's a bit of a war historian and the closing sentences rang a false note with him: "They could even use Bren guns. I liked the weapon. I saw it perform efficiently in the second World War in the jungles of Burma." Pete didn't immediately recognise the name of the ex-chairman of the North Western Fishery Board as being Japanese ... Nonetheless, it was an amusing note on which to conclude proceedings and go our separate ways, each with his own image of the impact on tourism in Connemara of units of the Irish army tearing up and down the coastline, loosing off salvoes at seals. "Peace In Our Time" seemed downright boring in comparison.

When invited to comment (my mistake) on the issue of the seals, Milady was of the view that the seals posed far less of a threat to the ecology, economy or environment that did those who lolled around in public houses in contemplation of such issues. Besides, her concert season was about to begin and those with time on their hands might condescend to publicise this fact by putting up posters in hotels and restaurants throughout the area. We agreed, naturally, never for a moment alluding to that other category of on-premise consumption that might have been overlooked. To smooth our path she would be talking about her season's programme on Connemara FM the very next day.

On a fine May morning you can smell the gorse and the hawthorn while driving the roads of Connemara, with the red and purple of the fuchsia now adding to the riot of colour transforming the countryside. And sure enough, at the appointed hour, Milady's initially diffident tones came across the airwaves, extolling the delights of her beloved Gothic chapel and exhorting all who would to share in the experience of pianos and violins, choirs and tenors. While it can be disconcerting to hear one's "significant other" disembodied through the ether, it's not nearly as off-putting as hearing recordings of one's own voice. "Good God. I don't sound like THAT! Do I?"

Ireland is music-mad. I knew this. But the extent of that madness and its manifestation in live performances only comes home when trying to find space to hang anything amid the welter of posters festooning the noticeboards in pubs and hotels. The restrained, tasteful Kylemore concert programme looked out of place amongst brightly-coloured blandishments to roll up to "Big Tom", "T. R. Dallas", "Mick Flavin & Philomena Begley", "The Saw Doctors" and "Susan McCann".

Our postering tour took us in a circle, more or less, around north Connemara—out to Cleggan, further out to Claddaghduff and then inwards again, following the coast to Clifden; everywhere a hive of activity, gearing up for the season that had effectively begun, but would not reach its peak for a full two months to come. The riot of colour that was the countryside was rivalled now by a summer scheme of Mediterranean hues, transforming weathered buildings into a pastel profusion, interspersed here and there with rectangles of a deeper shade; a man-made mirror of the landscape. If colour alone could influence climate, then Clifden bade to become the cote d'azur.

We continued south to Ballyconneely, until recently an outpost and now transformed by the magnetic appeal of the golf links on nearby Aillebrack. Alcock and Brown would have landed on Aillebrack, instead of pitching into Derrygimla bog, had they known of the existence of this natural aerodrome at the time. Its claims to become Europe's transatlantic airport were subsequently extolled by councillors and TDs of all persuasions—to no avail. Shannon became that transatlantic staging post, while Connemara continued to cry in vain for help to keep her people—her life's blood—at home. Maybe Ballyconneely has the last laugh. After all, a golf course is an infinitely more agreeable neighbour than an airport.

That once-barren tract stretching from Ballyconneely to Roundstone is barren no longer, dotted now with colourful cottages, spick-and-span symbols of an affluence hitherto unknown, undreamed of. Our midday destination was O'Dowd's, overlooking what must be the most painted harbour in the whole of Ireland, with its constant comings and goings of Galway hookers, glotógs and pucauns. Pete is in his seventh heaven. A lifelong subscriber to the "See Food" diet, (see food and eat it!), he can gorge himself on mussels, crab, lobster and salmon. The only thing known about BSE in Roundstone is that it may induce BES, but the link is unproven as yet.

Guarding the eastern approach to Roundstone is a substantial house that dates from the creation of the village by Alexander Nimmo around 1820. An auxiliary workhouse in Famine times, it had more recently been the summer home of that magical novelist Kate O'Brien, who christened it "The Fort". She chose the name well, for there is an aura of foreboding about this house behind the high protective wall. I cannot pass this place without a shudder of recollection. More than thirty years ago I was offered a bed there for the night, following a dance in the village hall, to which we teenagers made our way from all over Connemara. The next morning my Sloane Ranger hostess enquired how I had slept. I told her, truthfully, that I had scarcely slept a wink, becoming in turn feverishly hot and frozen to the marrow, terrified throughout, for no reason that I could fathom.

My svelte hostess exchanged glances with her older brother. "Come on. It's only fair we tell him. OK?" The brother was non-committal. Ignoring him, she explained that they had only recently acquired the house and were only gradually coming to learn of the stories that linked to it in the locality. One of these concerned the bedroom assigned to me, as guinea-pig. The story went that two doctors had carried out a suicide pact in the room, since when nobody had ever managed to get a night's sleep in it. Unemotional, pragmatic, quintessentially English, brother and sister had calmly continued eating their breakfast.

As we wound our way through Toombeola, past Ballynahinch and then along the Inagh Valley, Pete wondered aloud about the "psychic phenomena" that find such ready acceptance in Irish culture. "Ee, in Yorkshire us wud be done for witchery!" he declared. Maybe, though Yorkshire is hardly devoid of its own superstitions. I mused that just in this area alone we have the monastic bell, the phantom currach, the phantom schooner, the old woman by the east gate of Kylemore and the ghostly nun walking the west avenue in the grounds of the abbey. The first three are harbingers of disaster.

Mannin Bay is where the monks' bell tolls, invariably foretelling tragedy for one at least of those who hear it. I know of one survivor, but her companion on that occasion died soon afterwards as a consequence of medical incompetence. Similarly, the disappearing currach, manned by two fishermen, makes invitingly for the beach, just around a headland, giving promise of fresh fish for sale. Those who hasten their footsteps in anticipation are invariably disappointed. There is no currach anywhere to be seen. It is not a lucky omen.

The schooner I have witnessed myself, as a schoolboy. A glamorous lady editor, widowed many years before, had come to stay on Heather Island with her only son, a lad a few years my senior called Alan. We had gone over to Maujer's in Sallerna, beyond Cleggan, to buy lobsters. Old Maujer was a Breton, with a price on his head from de Gaulle's government. In involuntary exile, he had set up a collection point—for all the world like submarine pens—to hold lobsters destined for the Parisian restaurant trade. While the adults chose their fish and negotiated the price, Alan and I surveyed the tossing waters of rainswept Cleggan Bay, not a day that any boat should be out. Suddenly, there she was, a two-masted barque, sails furled, running into Cleggan, to ride out the pending storm, we surmised. She swept out of sight behind a headland. Curious to get another glimpse, we ran along the lane to see her re-emerge. She never did. My father, who had an answer to most queries, was strangely tight-lipped on this one.

Back in boarding school, I got a letter from home saying that Alan had been found dead, with his head in the gas oven of his room in college. On his desk was an unfinished essay on the philosophies of Albert Camus. At the bottom of the page Alan had written: "What is the point of it all?" By morbid coincidence—if indeed "coincidence" is the word—Alan's father had taken his own life in the same manner, something Alan never knew, so his grieving mother felt certain.

Pete was appalled. "It's the Celtic melancholy coming out in you, Irish!" That settled it. More railway line hardship for this infidel. The next day that promised fair, but not too fine, we'd walk the stretch from Recess to Oughterard. And we could be selective, for most of the permanent way from Recess to Maam Cross either runs beside the road or has been overlaid by the road. We could start walking from Bunscanniff, site of what was once "Flynn's Halfway House", a legend amongst 19th-century travellers for its discomforts. Just across the road, overlooking a small cutting, is one of the huts erected in 1891 to house some of the army of labourers employed on the construction of the permanent way. The huts had a short-term purpose, while the railway was intended to endure. The line's long since gone; and the huts remain.

The line ran along the northern shore of Lough Shindilla, well away from the present road on the southern shore, giving us pilgrims a certain state of detachment as we strolled, removed but not isolated, to the point where the old line traversed the road from Maam Cross to Maam Bridge. The station beyond this crossing was later converted into a factory, processing seaweed into fertiliser; to the detriment of its architectural appeal.

Our passage was both easy and interesting—for the line bisects the road at only one point—until we reached "The Quiet Man Bridge" at Leam, where old "Cannon Ball" once held sway, and now lies buried. Thereafter the going got very rough, repeatedly interrupted by broken bridges and rushing rivers. Sore and weary were we on eventually reaching Oughterard, the only worthwhile experience en route being the 700-foot cutting just short of the town. Walter Macken, Galwegian historical novelist and playwright, used delight in bringing his students and admirers to view this imposing physical feature, citing it as the great symbol of hope for the people of Connemara—their first inland link with the outside world.

Subsequent attempts to walk the remainder of the once-permanent way from Oughterard through Roscahill and Moycullen into Galway were similarly frustrated by a combination of impenetrable undergrowth, land reclamation and broken bridges. So we never did find the sunken motorbus that is said to lie in Ross Lake. Maurice Semple, who had written so comprehensively about Lough Corrib and its environs, regaled me with the story. Following the abrupt closure of the Galway—Clifden line in April 1935 and the swift removal of the running rails, an enterprising French travel company determined to explore the potential of a dedicated tour bus route along the permanent way, seeing that all the bridges were still intact, even if the railbed itself was badly in need of repair. The intrepid Frenchmen boarded their motor coach and set out from Galway station. The occupants returned, but their coach did not—abandoned to its watery grave in the depths of Ross Lake.

Was there really a book to be had out of this ill-fated railway line, this "symbol of hope" for the denizens of Connemara, so painstakingly constructed, so ruthlessly terminated? Well, there's a book in everything (and everybody!), but whether the history of a vanished local railway was the money spinner I needed just now was open to question. Not so to Pete. "Be sure to entitle it 'Via bloody Dolorosa' and dedicate it to Pete the Pilgrim!"

June

L ike Percy Bysshe Shelley almost two hundred years earlier, Jan Voske had disappeared into the "fainting air". To Prince Hal he had sent a note of apology and exculpation, declaring that he must sacrifice all for the sake of his art, blithely overlooking the fact that his voyage of self-discovery had been pre-paid by his princely patron. If *A Sea-grey House* were not to come naked into this world, something would have to be done ... Drawing on his encyclopaedic knowledge of foreign talent in the environs of that "town of the stranger", as Galway translates from the Gaelic tongue, Prince Hal commissioned Tamora, this time with gratifying results.

Tamora's moody masterpiece depicts the "long long house in the ultimate land of the undiscovered west," where, "islands and mountainous mainland share in a final reconciliation at this, the world's end." That the author is portrayed as a dissolute plantation proprietor on some exotic Caribbean island only enhances the air of whimsy that pervades "Ireland's only stress free zone". That tortuous path from fragmentary manuscript to finished volume, twice trodden now, could be undertaken again and again.

All of that lay in the mists of uncertain future, invisibly shaped by random pieces of one's past. Our recent past now caught up upon us in the form of a surprise visit from my erstwhile boss in the Macau Jockey Club. Lured from a plum post in the Australian racing hierarchy by a salary on which he could comfortably retire, this misfortunate had taken up office in Macau only to realise that those who had brought him in to oust another faction had themselves been ousted in the interim. Powerless and disillusioned, he had resigned, taking a world tour with his worried wife before returning to resurrect his career in his native Australia. His wife's innate nervousness had been further aggravated by an indiscriminate machine gun attack on the foyer of the posh new hotel in which they had been living in Macau. Their visit was timely, for their reaction to Heather Island was one of incredulity. "Who could ever have gone to work in Macau when they had such a paradise as this to enjoy?" Waverers along life's path need such timely reassurances.

Over many late night libations Ray and I tried to discern what it was about Macau that drew virtually everyone who had worked there back, and back again. If it wasn't the climate, the lifestyle or the money, could it be a sense of refuge, asylum even? Without reaching any conclusion, we could at least agree that neither of us would ever be found crossing the yawning mouth of the Pearl River again, whatever the bait.

June, as we were now to discover, is the start of the "open season" in Connemara, when anyone may materialise and anything can happen. Alone (as I genuinely believed) on Heather Island one sunny morning, chatting idly on the telephone to a favourite female, I was alerted to the onset of intruders by Teal and Plover barking a welcome as opposed to a warning. Three men appeared through the canopy of linden leaves that overhung the courtyard. They introduced themselves as a film crew, doing a location shoot for a documentary on the Galway–Clifden railway line. Danny Coulthard, persuasive producer of this series on vanished Irish railway lines, had, in his irrefutable way, secured such a confrontation, though without declaring it invasive.

Gradually the mystery became resolved. No, they hadn't thought that Heather Island formed any part of the long-vanished railway line, twelve miles north of Clifden as it lies. It was simply that in the course of filming along the route they had discovered that I held a wealth of research material relating to the old line. Even as we chatted the young Australian director fell hopelessly in love with his surroundings and promptly decided that he would shoot a portion of his film in these sylvan surroundings. As to how they had crossed the lake ... Simple. The old Culfin Anglers' boat. "But there are no oars or thole-pins in that boat." "No problem, matey, we took up the floorboards and used them as paddles." So much for my imagined island security.

Thus did I find myself in the totally spurious role of railway buff, historian, economist and political commentator, spouting inanities to camera in the utterly implausible setting of the lawn and drawingroom of my so-called hideaway. The results subsequently appeared on both RTE and BBC, bringing the predictable wave of derogatory remarks, many of them incorporating the word "chancer". Definitely grounds for not proceeding with that book on the railway.

In keeping with her "executive" status in Kylemore Abbey, Milady had forsaken her bicycle for a natty little black BMW. This improvement in her material comforts allowed me the luxury of evening strolls to join her at the Trading Post; exactly four miles from the boathouse to the bar. Not only did this pleasant discipline afford a degree of daily exercise, but it induced a delightful thirst as well. The trudge from the shore through Tully village and up the hill to Tullycross betokened one pint. The long, sweeping descent to Derryinver bridge warranted a second and the steep hills that lay in wait beyond surely justified a third such libation. Any surplus infusions must be left to chance, odds-on in Letterfrack in summer.

As Milady's duties delayed her departure from Kylemore

more often than not, ample opportunities arose to exchange news, views and gossip with both regulars such as Malcolm, Geoffrey, Alastair, Kraken, the collective "Gerries" and their womenfolk. Moreover, there was always the intriguing prospect of unexpected visitors, both native and foreign. In fact there are few greater pleasures that sitting supping in the evening sunshine watching the world go by in convivial company. Any lingering sense of purpose or urgency soon drifts into that insidious file marked "mañana".

Just as it began to appear that our idyllic existence in Connemara—on the western periphery of the last great wilderness in Europe (as Tom McGurk would have it)—had begun to outrun its tether of meaningful existence, several events conspired to cajole us into continuing our sojourn in the wild, wild west. Prime amongst pares was Milady's burgeoning career in the Byzanthine scheming of Kylemore Abbey Inc. This would stand her in good stead whether in Washington, Whitehall or Wexford town. It was, I thought, about time that the boot of "breadwinner" should be surreptitiously shifted from male to female. Furthermore, I had in my head this mischievous contention of Grandfather Gogarty's either to prove or gainsay. Belligerent as he had been in all his manifestations, Gogarty had gone into print as saying that the female orgasm was not only dangerous but downright harmful, inducing otherwise inexplicable pains and aches and—in extreme instances—abdominal adhesions. It seemed to me, looking about, that such proving grounds as these were unlikely to be surpassed

The keys to this particular form of anthropology were fishwives—as I had come to think of Juicy and Lucy; following my dim-witted realisation that they were two rather than one. Surely twelve months' social intercourse had created sufficient intimacy to permit at least tentative overtures on topics of this kind? By now helplessly beguiled by Connemara and its curious mixture of cant and candour, attributable in part at least to constant closeness to the elements—an almost primal existence—I had come to think of our adoptive habitat as being much more cosmopolitan that simply rural. The combined influences of emigration, immigration and the lasting effects of increasingly intensive tourism had stripped Connemara of virtually all the quiet, unruffled rural humdrum that still persists in inland agricultural counties where tourism is as yet in its infancy, with minimal economic significance.

The problem with pursuing such investigations as I had in mind lay in those afore-mentioned unexpected encounters. On one sunny evening, as a crowd of us "cocktail drinkers" sat sipping and gossiping on the cut stone wall across the road from the Trading Post, discussing plans for a Midsummer Night's celebration, a stranger approached me, introducing himself as Paul Gogarty, a cousin.

Obeying the local convention that forbids such occurrences as this to interfere with the general hum of conversation by the formality of introductions, I drew the stranger to one side. Credentials were necessary, for I had no cousin by that name. An explanation was in order. "Mary Gogarty was my great-grandmother. Her lover—father of my grandfather—absconded, so Mary Gogarty gave her son her own surname. That's how I'm your cousin. I'm here to find my roots. Oh, I'm also the travel writer for the *Daily Telegraph*."

"Fair enough, if you say. But who was this Mary Gogarty. I never heard of anyone of that name in my mother's immediate family."

"Mary was Oliver St. John Gogarty's sister, and that's for certain!" Here was a mystery, for the bould Oliver had only one sister, and her name was Mayflo. The stranger's frown of determination suddenly brightened, as his eyes met mine with Gogarty's piercing, ice-blue gaze.

"Don't you get it? Mayflo was simply an elision of Mary and

Florence. I'm still right. I knew it. I had to be right!"

Fair enough. I had another cousin, or perhaps my children had, for a genealogical chart would have Paul on the same tier as them, notwithstanding that he was almost an exact contemporary of mine. We saw quite a lot of Paul and his family over the coming days, as he composed his feature article for the *Daily Telegraph*. It duly appeared some months subsequently, capturing not only the atmosphere of Connemara, but disclosing Paul's gnawing anxiety to discover his lineage and his profound relief at having finally done so.

Having whetted our family's appetite for skeletons in the cupboard, our new-found cousin professed himself reluctant to pursue the matter further, politely resisting the notion that the evidence, as it emerged, pointed strongly to his being a direct descendant not of Mayflo, but of the bould Oliver himself. Enough, he averred, in this instance was as good as a feast. When pressed on the subject he expressed fears that even a little learning was a dangerous thing, bringing to mind a snatch of dialogue from one of our forebear's lesser known books, *Going Native*.

"Now you little morosoph, you know very well that you are keeping me in suspense with all this cross-word business instead of ..."

"Who's a little morosoph?"

"You are a little morosoph."

"What's a little morosoph?"

"It's a person with a clear head who follows foolish pursuits."

Come to think of it, that word morosoph, absent from many dictionaries, could be held to apply much closer to home than to newly discovered kith or kin. On no account must Milady be apprised of such a pertinent term of potential approbation. By now those notions of deriving worthwhile income from either the island or the lake had begun to wear thin. No, not just thin—threadbare. The realisation was disillusioning; dissipation of a dream. Once again writing for reward presented itself as the only pretext for remaining in these idyllic surroundings.

Some hold that writing is the one truly transportable art, in that it can be undertaken anywhere, even in gaol. If that were so, how much more inspirational my own circumstances? Having rowed Milady ashore each morning I had the island to myself, with only Teal, Plover and the anonymous cats for company. The view from my study window should be conducive to that dream-like trance in which thoughts feel free to enter, swirl and tumble in the subconscious before taking some definitive form capable of being committed to paper. Through a frame of laburnum and escalonia on the left, roses and rhododendrons to the right, I could let my dreaming gaze wander across "that great rock", where the woolly locusts steadfastly consume the landscape. This pastoral idyll is occasionally punctured by a solitary motorcar climbing across the scene, rising in tandem with my impecuniousness it sometimes seemed.

In the foreground the swifts dart across the lake; low when rain looms, higher when it does not. The mallard, having reared their young, resume their carefree cruising, while the swans seem to have gone off the idea of procreation, spending too much time away from the islet where they had shown signs of nesting. The cawing ravens, screeching seagulls and prehistoric herons manage to ignore each other's existence for the most part, uniting in indignation only when the cormorant reappears, skimming low across the water to alight on his favoured rock, wings held wide to dry.

The truth of the matter, if I were honest (which exercise invariably necessitates the prefix "brutally"), was not difficult to comprehend, once the desire for that comprehension manifested itself. A child could have grasped it. Wallowing in the self-indulgence of converting this "rookery" from holiday house to permanent home I had spoiled myself to a point whereby I could neither live to work nor work to live. It was a chastening realisation. The winter had been one long obsession with the elements and our capacity to cope with them. And now the summer seductively invited me to succumb to the hedonism of holiday-making. Life was quite simply too damned good to allow any form of disciplined endeavour to interfere. I could bluff and feign and dissimulate, but I would not win. Unpalatable as this confrontation between the "ego" and the "meum" had been, I felt immensely relieved for having undergone it.

In previous instances this catharsis had invariably proved the prelude to yet another change of career. So, whither now? Well, nowhere just yet anyway. After all, our first summer as residents on Heather Island had been entirely consumed with renovations; from Robinson Crusoe through Heath Robinson. While in winter the candles in the window had hardly been in imitation of Mary Robinson, to whom such artifices were more symbolic than essential.

The commencement of the three-month school holidays afforded another excuse to defer draconian decisions. In Milady's daily absences it fell to me to resume the role of parenting. This inevitably involved a great deal of ferrying the twins hither, thither and yon, for they were of course too young to drive and few of their friends and acquaintances lived within reasonable cycling distance. Moreover, the Connemara roads in summer became just too thronged to make cycling anything less than hazardous. Over the weeks we made forays to those other inhabited islands that lie off the coast of Connemara— Inisturk, Inisbofin and Clare, as well as to Omey, accessible on foot at low tide.

In addition to the invigoration of summer boat trips on the Atlantic there is a wonderful feeling of escapism experienced in a day spent on an offshore island; all cares and concerns left firmly on the quayside in Cleggan. Here lies Hyperthuleana — beyond the beyonds — the realisation that the last great wilderness in Europe is also but the launching pad for a grandeur of isolation that is even greater still. Wandering those narrow, stone-walled lanes that enclose pocket handkerchiefs of fields, serenaded by the larks, lost in nostalgic enjoyment of flora and fauna long since obliterated from the mainland, provides a perspective of weightlessness and timelessness through which to view the distant mainland, where the Twelve Bens can appear — should you wish — to represent those burdens of everyday terrestrial existence, temporarily relinquished.

Returning one evening from such an expedition the twins and I dropped anchor outside the Trading Post, where it seemed that everyone we knew in the neighbourhood and many more besides had assembled in the evening sunshine, imbibing and chatting animatedly. Well, one could hardly pass by. Within moments the twins had discerned the reason and reported back excitedly.

"Dad, it's all happening right here! We can stay, can't we? Please, please! All the other kids are going to come too."

"Easy now. What's the story?"

"Midsummer's night, that's what! There's this monster party, just over there in front of the Connemara West buildings. Bonfire, bar-b-que, bands and — Dad — booze!"

Holy Moses, was it Midsummer's night already? The summer had barely begun and already it had reached its apex. Could the days really be going to shorten from now on. Why couldn't time ever stand still, just once in a while? Falling in readily with this prospect of communal celebration, Milady made but one stipulation. We must first go back to the island (our island), for she needed to change and, besides, I was expecting a visitor, know it or not ... and he was due for dinner.

My mystery caller turned out to be the amiable but insistent Danny Coulthard. He had journeyed from afar to deliver this proposal, one I simply must accept. Wheedling, cajoling, forceful and humorous as he felt his delivery demanded, Danny would not accept no as an answer. Not indeed that his proposition ever seriously risked rejection, offering as it did an intriguing mixture of research, script writing, travel and narration.

"Danny, this all sounds too good to be true, as long as it wouldn't mean having to leave here. Would it?" Milady and the twins held their collective breath. Was Dad going to blow it? Would he bite the hand that offered to feed not just him, but them as well? They stared, now at me, then at Danny, veritable deus ex machina, wonder worker, alchemist, wizard, liberator … Poker player that he is, Danny simply smiled and apologised for having to rush away, the more so as he was missing what was clearly going to be "the mother of all parties", by which some at least were meant to understand the festivities in Letterfrack.

Midsummer's night in Letterfrack fulfilled its promise. On a balmy summer night, with not even a breeze to rustle the leaves on the sycamores that flanked the green, the bonfire blazed superfluously into the barely darkened sky, as the band played and the drink flowed. Kraken's trumpet blared, sometimes in support, and sometimes in solo celebration, like some disembodied Pied Piper exhorting further frenzy. The carnival transcended all castes, creeds and factions, prompting even piscatorial Stuart Feakes to suspend his feud with the fish farmers, as he exchanged utterly implausible assertions with Geoffrey and Malcolm, Gerry Fish and Edwin, that Mannin Bay business a thing of the past for now.

The impromptu, makeshift outdoor bar counter, manned in turn by Culfin stalwarts Malachy Kane, Phelim O'Flaherty and Cathal Heanue proved as powerful a magnet for the adults as did the music to the youngsters. Lewis, his curfew lifted for this evening, appointed himself major domo of the drinkers, exchanging badinage and epithets as the occasion demanded. Batman, Gerry Park and Gerry Sheep ensured Lewis a succession of soft targets, to his wife's smiling approval. Oisín, swathed now in reflective sash and armbands, attempted to elicit a promise of a lift home from Alastair, still in his chef's gear after a late stint in Rosleague, egged on by guffaws from Terry, between drags on his perennial, half-smoked cheroot. On the periphery the "Squire", "Sam Sailor" and "Some like it Hot" had struck up in competition to the pop band, with Kraken as occasional accompanist on his wanderings through the throng.

Shane Ruane, his brother Paud and their respective spouses had come up from Tully, as, independently, had Martin Golden and Thady Hurley with their families. Milady's workmates from Kylemore Abbey were also resolved to make this a night to remember, even if it meant paying the penalty the following day. While the Trading Post was hardly a "Hemingway" haunt, he materialised nonetheless, assiduously attending to the demands of his frail but determined landlady, Mary Sammon. Bernice was an absentee, but then I had never encountered her in such a setting, where she was in any case represented by work colleagues, Donal, the shopkeeper and his brother Brendan, the butcher.

As that deathless evening wore on more and more surprises materialised, notably Prince Hal, flanked by both Falstaff and Bottom, alternately minders and jesters to that peer of the merchant realm, though of the truant Jan Voske there was no evidence, bandaged or otherwise. Mark, the marksman, and Michael Gibbons were deep in conversation on the latest in Michael's unending series of archaeological discoveries, attracting, briefly, the rapt attentions of Juicy and Lucy, along with the trumpet widow.